THE ESSEX HUNDRED HISTORIES

100 EVENTS AND PERSONALITIES THAT SHAPED THE NATION'S HISTORY

With National and International Timelines

*Andrew Summers
and John Debenham*

*Illustrated by
Elizabeth Summers*

www.essex100.com

Published by Essex Hundred Publications
Rutland House
90 – 92 Baxter Avenue
Southend-on-Sea
Essex SS2 6HZ
www.essex100.com

The Essex Hundred Histories
This new edition first published September 2015
Written by Andrew Summers and John Debenham
Illustrated by Elizabeth Summers
© Copyright Andrew Summers and John Debenham
September 2015
Reprinted January 2018 (with changes)
Reprinted November 2018 (with changes)
All rights reserved.

A catalogue record for this book is available from
The British Library.
ISBN 9780993108310

Typeset by Hutchins Creative Limited
Printed by 4edge Publishing
22a Eldon Way
Eldon Way Industrial Estate
Hockley Essex SS5 4AD

CONTENTS

The King of Bling

INTRODUCTION

From the Romans to nuclear power and the space shuttle: how and why has Essex played such a pivotal role in the development of British history? Some interesting facts and unusual events make up the remarkable history of Essex. Daniel Defoe, the great English novelist, wrote in his book, "A Tour through the whole Island of Great Britain",

"I set out, the 3rd of April 1722, passing Bow-Bridge where the county of Essex begins."

Essex is one of our oldest counties and derives its name from the sixth century kingdom of the East Saxons. It is naturally bounded by rivers: Thames to the south, Lea to the west, Stour to the north and to the east by the North Sea (formerly called the German Ocean). It remained virtually unchanged for nearly 1,500 years from its emergence as a county or autonomous region until local government reorganisation in 1965. This meant the loss of the south western corner of the county to create the London Boroughs of Waltham Forest, Redbridge, Newham, Barking and Havering. Nevertheless, for the purpose of this book, 'Essex' is taken to mean the 'Natural County' of pre-1965 and as far back as Roman times.

What is the *Hundred* and where did the name come from? It is fair to say that there is no definitive consensus among historians. The *Hundred* and its subdivision the *hide* are measurements of land. They grew out of a tribal organisation of land holdings where the *hide* was a piece of land capable of supporting a family, which could mean an extended family of fifty people or so.

The *Hundred* was a natural progression to a larger administrative area consisting of *100 hides*. In time it came to be a subdivision of a county or shire, having its own court and the power to settle local disputes. It was as late as 1867 that the Hundred Court was supplanted by the County Court in the County Courts Act. The *Hundred*, as an administrative entity, lasted from Saxon times until it was replaced by the modern urban, borough and district councils of the early twentieth century.

The *Hundred* was formalised as a fiscal unit in the eleventh century by William the Conqueror. Twenty years after the Battle of Hastings, in 1086, Norman England was stable enough for William to be able to send out Royal Commissioners to, in effect, catalogue the nation, using the system of *Hundreds*. This resulted in the *Domesday Book*, the first national asset register. Used to settle property disputes, usually in favour of the ruling Normans, this register was, much more importantly for William, a basis for the efficient collection of taxes. It could be said that the Normans were the first to introduce taxation on an organised basis.

There is a view that *Hundred* in Saxon England was just a translation from the Roman (Latin) 'Centurion'. The Centurion was the officer supposedly commanding one hundred men known as the Centuria. This view however would seem unlikely since the Centuria rarely consisted of 100 men and frequently had only eighty. Other explanations include the term *Hundred* being the land area that, in times of trouble, could raise a force of a hundred men bearing arms. Alternatively areas of land termed *Hundreds* may have incorporated several villages or settlements controlled simply by councils of 100 men. The English word hundred has German origins although it is possible England may even have exported the term *Hundred*, as a land area, to Scandinavia and northern Germany where the *Hundred* was also used as an administrative land area. In Sweden it was known as the 'Härad', in Denmark the 'Herred' and in Germany as the 'Harde'. On the other hand it may be that the *Hundred* arrived in England from Germany via Scandinavia with the Viking or Saxon invaders. Whatever the explanation, it is known that by the time of Alfred the Great an administrative system of *Hundreds* was widely in use.

The one hundred or more topics we have taken from the history of Essex, as with most histories, revolve around people of strong character: the good, the bad, the eccentric, perhaps the unbelievable and the just plain unlucky. Many have had profound effects on wider national, and sometimes international, histories. The 'good' would include the Leigh fishermen who so unselfishly sailed their 'Little Ships of Leigh' to Dunkirk and 'The Lady on the Five Pound Note', Elizabeth Fry, who from her home in East Ham worked tirelessly for prison reform. The 'bad' were such as Hempstead's ruthlessly evil Dick Turpin whose cries of, 'Stand and Deliver!' were heard all over the county and Baron Richard Riche of Leez Priory who, in a BBC History Magazine poll, was nominated the worst Briton of the 16th century. For 'eccentricity' we may look to Dunmow's Lionel Lukin who, on inventing the unsinkable lifeboat, tested it in the village 'Doctor's Pond'. As for the 'plain unlucky' James Cook of Witham was convicted and subsequently hanged for a series of fires; some that occurred while he was in gaol. Was ever a woman of strong character more unlucky than Rochford's Ann Boleyn who lost her head just through being unable to produce a son!

For the 'unbelievable' we have the Essex "George and the Dragon" tale from Wormingford, implausible ghost stories from Borley and perhaps the most amazing of all, the supposition that most of the works of William Shakespeare were in fact penned by an Essex Man, Edward de Vere of Castle Hedingham. For convenience we have separated the book into two time periods. For each of these we have included a timeline to give a global background to what was happening in Essex.

ACKNOWLEDGEMENTS

Essex Hundred Histories has been our most successful publication to date. It has been reprinted several times since it was first published in 2008. However, although we are loath to make change for the sake of change, we felt a new edition was justified. Our research over the last few years has uncovered many new 'facts'. New chapters have been added and the existing ones updated. In our opinion this new book is better than ever. Where possible we have kept the original opening poetic lines taken from our very first book the *Essex Hundred* and have even added some new ones.

Bringing a title such the *Essex Hundred Histories* to publication requires a huge amount of research and has taken us to all parts of the county and sometimes further afield. We have received help and encouragement from churchwardens, curators, archivists, editors, librarians, the press office of Ford Motor Company and many others. Without them the book would not have been possible and we are indebted to them. Special thanks are due to our wives, Greg Debenham and Glenis Summers, who have provided support throughout, and made some incisive observations when they were most needed. We are once again indebted to Elizabeth Summers for her excellent illustrations. The only exception is the drawing of Essex Farm Cemetery shown on page 150 which is credited to an unknown artist with the initials EM.

The valuable work that many local historians undertake is often copied and quoted in other media without credit or reference back to the source material. We have tried to make our bibliography (Page 208) as comprehensive as possible and have acknowledged quotations or direct contributions in the text. In-depth historical research requires the skills of a forensic detective in following leads and the patience of a saint to spend many hours in record offices or libraries whether studying archive material or simply collections of memorabilia such as old postcards. Criss-crossing the county our investigations have been interesting and enlightening but above all enjoyable. The list of places and contact addresses at the end of the book is included in order to help any reader wishing to explore further. To those that do so, we wish you well and hope that you gain as much pleasure from your efforts as we have had in researching for the book.

Andrew Summers
John Debenham

*Boudica's monument on the river Thames opposite
the House of Parliament in Westminster*

TIMELINE

ESSEX EVENT	AD	NATIONAL or INTERNATIONAL EVENT
	43	*Romans Invade England*
Boudicca sacks Colchester	60	*London designated capital of Britain*
Kingdom of the East Saxons founded	500	*Mohammad captures Mecca*
Harold interred at Waltham Abbey	1066	*Battle of Hastings*
Guernons become Monfichet	1071	*Norman invasion of Ireland*
Robert Fitzwalter leads the rebels	1215	*Magna Carta sealed at Runnymede*
Castle Hedingham falls to King John	1216	*King John succeeded by Henry III*
Edward III stays in Boxted	1354	*Birth of Owen Glendower*
Peasants revolt begins in Brentwood	1381	*Peasants revolt ends at Smithfield*
First Pie Powder Court in Essex	1398	*Teutonic Order occupies Gotland*
Richard Wright wins 'Dunmow Flitch'	1345	*Birth of Sandro Botticelli*
Edmund Tudor leaves Barking Abbey	1441	*Eton College founded*
Henry Marney supports Henry Tudor	1485	*Richard III dies at Bosworth Field*
Ann Boyleyn beheaded	1536	*Michaelangelo paints Sistine Chapel*
Hadleigh Castle sold to Lord Rich	1552	*St Andrews Golf Club founded*
'Baron' Riche founds Felsted School	1564	*Birth of William Shakespeare*
Harbingers inspect Mark Hall in Harlow	1576	*Martin Frobisher explores Canada*
Walden becomes Saffron Walden	1582	*Pope Gregory XIII announces New Style (Gregorian) calendar*
Queen Elizabeth I speaks in Tilbury	1588	*Spanish Armada defeated*
	1603	*Death of Queen Elizabeth I*
Canvey Dutch Cottage built	1618	*Sir Walter Raleigh is executed*
	1621	*James I dies, Charles I becomes king*
Matthew Hopkins charges Elizabeth Clarke of Manningtree with witchcraft	1644	*Abel Tasman maps north east of Australia (as New Holland)*
	1649	*Charles I is executed*
Samuel Pepys elected MP for Harwich	1685	*Judge Jeffreys holds bloody Assizes*
Daniel Defoe opens a brickworks	1694	*Bank of England is founded*
Birth of Dick Turpin	1705	*Construction of Blenheim Palace*
Walton Tower built	1721	*Robert Walpole becomes first prime minister of Britain*
First recorded race at Galleywood	1770	*Birth of poet William Wordsworth*
Tide Mill constructed at Battlesbridge	1775	*American revolution begins*
Richard Rigby investigated	1781	*First building society in Birmingham*
Eliab Harvey takes change of 'fencibles'	1798	*Irish insurrection defeated*

The ENIGMA OF BOADICEA

Boadicea, her Latin name, or Boudicca, her Celtic name, is one of Britain's greatest heroines. Her statue, triumphantly driving her chariot, stands on the Thames Embankment by Westminster Bridge, opposite the Houses of Parliament. She is remembered for her battles against the occupying Romans nearly 2,000 years ago.

In AD 59-60 following the death of her husband, Prasutagus, the King of the Iceni, Queen Boadicea and the Iceni rebelled against an increasingly repressive Roman rule. The occupiers had broken nearly all of their promises and humiliated Boadicea's family. Fired up with rage, Boadicea led an avenging army to attack Roman Colchester (Camulodunum) totally destroying the town and killing all its inhabitants. The queen's forces then swept south-westward across Essex to burn and sack London (Londinium) which was undefended since the Roman garrison was fighting in Wales. Shortly afterward Boadicea went on to mete out the same fate to Roman St. Albans (Verulamium).

Archaeological evidence is conclusive that Colchester, London and St Albans were destroyed and burned to the ground about 2,000 years ago. Evidence of the burning survives in what is known as 'Boudicca's Destruction Horizon'. Excavations in all three locations have revealed a thick layer of red soot, as well as artefacts showing evidence of severe scorching. There is a glass panel in the cellar of the George Hotel in the High Street, Colchester, through which can be seen the distinctive burnt red clay.

After destroying St Albans (Verulamium) Boadicea's army moved northwards, but over confident and undisciplined, they fell into a carefully laid trap set by the, now highly organised, Roman Commander Suetonius Paulinus. The Britons were annihilated and the revolt was over. To avoid capture Boadicea is thought to have killed herself by taking poison. The site of this final battle has led to much speculation. Battle sites have been suggested as far apart as Staffordshire, Cambridge, Worcester the Midlands, Surrey and even London's Kings Cross. One popular myth suggested that Boadicea is buried under platform 8 or 9 at Kings Cross Station! Where Boadicea's forces made their final stand remains a mystery. To date no mass graves, supposedly containing the remains of up to 80,000 bodies and their weapons that might confirm the battle's location have been unearthed.

All known records of Boadicea's revolt have come from Roman sources written at least 40 years after the event. Thus all the 'facts' on Queen Boadicea's revolt are from the 'victors' second hand accounts which, over the centuries, have been translated, reinterpreted and retranslated several times, sometimes inaccurately and with large parts missing.

Much of the romantic myth surrounding Boadicea was created by the Victorians. It is exemplified by Thomas Thornycroft's statue, of a triumphant Boadicea and daughters in her chariot. Thornycroft died in 1885 and the statue was erected 17 years later. Boadicea's attack on Colchester is well documented as is the assault on London. What is questionable is the size of her army and how it travelled from Colchester to London. When was it and how long did it take? Was it in long days of dry summer or short wet winter days?

The Roman chronicler Tacitus records Boadicea's Army as initially numbering 100,000 and doubling en-route to London. Travelling overland from Colchester to London for an army of this size would have been a huge logistical exercise. Essex, largely forested, had no roads that could accommodate such numbers. Every single river, and there were many, would have presented a major obstacle. Closer to London the problems would have been even greater. The Rivers Roding and Lea would have been exceedingly difficult to cross for the army with their fighting chariots, baggage wagons and hundreds of pack animals. In Roman times these rivers grew and shrank with the tides or seasons over wide flood plains.

It is conceivable that the vanguard of Boadicea's Army could have arrived at London while the rearguard was leaving Colchester 60 miles away. Records indicate Boadicea's decision to attack London was made in the heat of the moment after the destruction of Colchester, i.e. no advanced planning was made.

The size of Boadicea's Army needs to be questioned. Roman chroniclers suggest the rebel force swelled to as high as 230,000. If this was the case, and based on an estimated population in England working backwards in time from the *Domesday Book* it would seem virtually the whole population of England would have been in Boadicea's Army!

Boadicea, Celtic queen, wife, mother and rebel, is destined, it would seem, to remain a legendary national heroine and yet a historical mystery.

KING OF BLING??

In a simple wooden coffin he was laid to rest
His eyes with two golden crosses were blest

In 2004, close to Priory Park in Southend, archaeologists, in advance of a proposed road widening scheme, made a surprise discovery - a complete and undefiled Saxon burial chamber dating from the early 7th century.

The only reliable history of this period is the *Ecclesiastical History of the English Peoples* completed by the benedictine monk, the Venerable Bede, in AD 731. In it he wrote of a King Saebert reigning over the East Saxons in AD 604. Saebert died in 616 and it is possible that it was his burial chamber that was discovered.

King Saebert, or Saebba as some call him, came to Christianity through his uncle Aethelbert, King of Kent. When he died it would seem that he desired to be buried as his faith required and was laid to rest in a simple wooden coffin, the only reference to his religion being two gold foil crosses that could have been laid on his eyes.

His sons, however, would appear to have had different ideas. Tired of being dominated by Christian Kent they rebelled against their father's faith and turned to traditional pagan practice.

To our good fortune the ideas of Saeward, Seaxred and Seaxbald, the king's sons prevailed. Their father was buried as befitted someone of his noble birth, wealth and status. Saebert was given everything he might need for his journey in the next life. The chamber was bedecked with, among other things, drinking vessels, cooking and eating utensils, valued personal possessions and weapons. Some of these items would have been hanging from iron hooks riveted to the walls but many were carefully arranged around the body. Music was not forgotten since remains were found of an instrument resembling a lyre.

The burial chamber has proved a treasure trove, throwing much light on early Saxon Essex. It has been said that it is the most important find since the graves at Sutton Hoo in Suffolk were excavated in the nineteen-eighties. Of the quality of the artefacts and the wealth and status of the occupant of this grave there can be no doubt. That it was indeed King Saebert must for the time being at least remain supposition since no actual body remained. It would seem though that to call whoever it was 'Southend's King of Bling', may not be wholly inappropriate.

THE CHAPEL OF ST PETER-on-the-WALL

From ruined Othona grew St Peter's-on-the-Wall
And St. Cedd its new Bishop, ministering to all.

In 654 St Cedd landed on the Essex coast at Bradwell-on-Sea, then called Ythancaestir. Invited by King Sigeberht to bring Christianity to his people, Cedd built a simple wooden church near the ruins of the old Roman fort of Othona.

In time, as his mission grew, he replaced this with the more solid Cathedral Church of St Peter using stone from the Roman ruins. The Chapel of St Peter-on-the-Wall is all that remains today but then the monastic community would have included a school, library, hospital and a guest house. From this base Cedd, as Bishop of the East Saxons, established Christian missions throughout Essex at Mersea, Tilbury, Prittlewell and Upminster. Upon his death from a plague, in about 664 St Peter's was taken into the diocese of London, St Paul's, and became a Minster for the surrounding country.

After the Norman invasion, and maybe as a consequence of it, in 1068 St Peter's became the property of the Benedictine Monastery of St Valerie-sur- Somme. It remained under French Benedictine control until 1391 when the estate was bought by Bishop William of Wykeham and brought into English jurisdiction.

As a religious community it flourished until its rapid decline in the seventeen hundreds. For many years after 1750 the chapel was used as a barn for storing grain and as a shelter for cattle. It was not to be used for religious purposes again until its restoration and re-consecration in 1920.

St Peter's Chapel is now once again part of the community life of Bradwell village. Regular services are held during the summer months. The chapel is open year round during daylight hours, providing visitors with a haven of quiet and shelter from the elements on this often bleak North Sea coast.

A short walk southward along the sea wall from St Peter's is 'The Othona Community'. It was founded by the Revd. Norman Motley, a former RAF chaplain, who wrote, after seeing St Peter's for the first time in 1946, "…the sense of thirteen centuries of prayer was almost overpowering…the moment I entered the building I knew we were home…." He went on to establish a religious community. Taking its name from the old Roman fort, the community, with its 'open to all' philosophy, continues to this day.

It could be said that St Cedd's surviving monument is St Peter's Chapel. It could also be said that his spirit lives on in the Othona community.

FIGHTING OFF THE VIKINGS

Beamfloete: Safe haven for Haesten the Black?
The Battle of Benfleet was to change all that.

In 892 the Danes mounted a large-scale attack on the England of Alfred the Great. The main fleet of 250 ships landed their 'Great Army' on the south coast of Kent and set up base near Ashford. At the same time the Viking chieftain, Haesten 'The Black', arrived in the Thames estuary with 80 ships. First settling in the village of Milton near Sheppey, Haesten was forced by Alfred to move across the Thames to the Danish settlement of Beamfleote; now South Benfleet. A Danish community had been established there for some years, working as shipwrights. It was also a perfect place from which to launch raids around the coast, into Kent and even up to London. It had fresh water from two streams and was surrounded by forest – the name Beamfleote meant wood and water. Hidden from the estuary's main stream, yet with easy access to the sea, tidal marshes prevented surprise attack from the water.

After strengthening the settlement's defences and mounting a garrison guard, Haesten set off on raiding activities further afield, leaving his wife and children behind. Meanwhile the original 'Great Army' was losing ground to King Arthur in the Weald of Kent. Elements of the Viking force, fearing defeat, escaped and made their way across the Thames to Benfleet to bolster the garrison there.

These developments alarmed King Alfred, still fighting the invaders in Wessex. His son Edward, together with brother-in-law Ethelflaed, raised a fresh army in London and marched east along the Thames valley keeping to forest tracks. Marshalling their forces on the high ground of Hadleigh, they swooped on the unsuspecting Danes at Benfleet, storming the fort. Haesten's men were routed. Many survivors fled overland to the Danelaw settlement at Shoebury but Haesten's wife and two children were captured and taken to London. With the fort vanquished, many of the Viking ships were burned. Later Alfred ordered the return to Haesten of his family, in exchange for his promise never again to attack England.

Archaeological surveys have pinpointed the probable site of the Viking ships' anchorage. It runs from the Canvey side of the Railway Bridge, through to the drainage streams of 'Church Creek' behind St Mary's Church and comes up behind the Anchor Pub to the back of 'The Moorings' Hall. It is the area from the railway bridge to the 'Hoy and Helmut' pub that is a likely site for the burning of the ships. As to Haesten's Fort, it is thought likely to have been built within the confines of the car park near Benfleet station, between School Lane and the High Street.

A stone sculpture by Anthony Lysycia, shown below, commemorates

The Battle of Benfleet and stands in the conservation area between Ferry Road and Benfleet Creek.

In terms of numbers engaged it was not a major battle. It was however decisive and marked the beginning of the end for the Danes in Essex. A few years later, in 895, a substantial force of Danish raiders was again outwitted by King Alfred who trapped their fleet at Ware by blocking the River Lea, thus establishing a lasting boundary for Essex. (see page 178)

Alfred died in 899. His legacy was a relatively peaceful England. His realm was roughly south of a line from Essex to the Mersey. The country north of this line, known as the Danelaw, negotiated by Alfred and the Danish leader Guthrum, was controlled by the Vikings. The peace was short lived.

In Essex things came to a head in 991 in the reign of King Aethelred at the Battle of Maldon. Anglo Saxons, under the command of Ealdorman Byrhtnoth and his thegns*, were defeated by Vikings, led by Olaf Tryggvason, at the Battle of Maldon. The Viking force of between two and four thousand vastly outnumbered the Anglo Saxons. Byrhtnoth was killed, as were most of the English nobility fighting with him. After the battle, King Aethelred, 'The Unready', agreed to buy off the Vikings with an estimated payment of more than 3,000kg of silver. This was supposedly the first instance of what became known as 'Danegeld'. In 2006, a nine feet high bronze statue of Byrhtnoth (right), by John Doubleday, was erected at the end of Maldon's Promenade, looking towards the battle site. Around its base are depicted scenes of the battle that was the beginning of the end of Anglo-Saxon rule.

Byrhtnoth

The end finally came in 1016 when Canute the Great (Cnut), King of Denmark and Norway, led a Viking army against the English, or Anglo-Saxon, army led by King Edmund II, Ironsides, at the Battle of Ashingdon. Following his heavy defeat, Edmund signed a treaty whereby all of England except Wessex would be ruled by Canute and when one of them died the other would become King of all England. Shortly after this, in November, Edmund died and Canute duly ruled the whole kingdom. Thus England became a single united kingdom.

The term 'Thegn' described either an aristocratic retainer of a king or nobleman in Anglo-Saxon England, or, as a class term, the majority of the aristocracy below the ranks of ealdormen and high-reeves.

NOT A LOT OF PEOPLE KNOW THAT!

Beside the present church building,
An inscription, on a stone lying flat,
Reads: 'HAROLD KING OF ENGLAND 1066'
Now - 'Not a lot of people know that!'

The earliest recorded history of Waltham Abbey goes back to King Canute. Towards the end of Canute's reign, in 1034, a blacksmith in the village of Montacute in Somerset discovered a large black flint cross. The cross was removed from the hill and placed in a wagon on the orders of Tovi, the Lord of Montacute, who was also a close advisor to the King. However the beasts (twelve red oxen and twelve white cows) pulling the wagon refused to move. There was much discussion as to what to do and Tovi addressed the crowd gathered around calling for suggestions. Someone shouted, 'Take it to Canterbury', another called 'Winchester' but the cart stood rooted to the ground. Tovi then remarked out loud that he was going back to Waltham, where he owned a hunting lodge on the banks of the River Lea, and all of a sudden the cart started to move and appeared to push the animals forward. The wagon, accompanied on its journey by a great throng of people from Montacute, continued non-stop until it reached Essex. Tovi saw it as a sign and decided to build a place of worship on the spot – now Waltham Abbey.

To honour the cross Tovi selected fine jewels to decorate it. However on attempting to fix them with nails to the right arm of the cross it was said that blood suddenly gushed out. Tovi was stunned by this happening. The jewels were immediately removed and placed in a small bag close by and the blood was kept in a silver goblet. Legend grew that just by touching the cross a miracle might happen and Waltham and its cross became a centre of pilgrimage and celebration.

In 1060 Harold Godwinson, Earl of Wessex and later to be the last Saxon King of England, consecrated a new, larger church on the site after apparently being cured of a paralysis there. Harold became King in January 1066, following the death of Edward the Confessor. Edward was alleged to have said to Harold on his deathbed, *I commend my wife and all my kingdom to your care*. Duke William of Normandy however disputed the succession. He asserted that Edward had told him virtually the same thing.

Although supported by most of the English nobility, King Harold soon had other problems to worry about. In September 1066 he had to fight off a large Viking force from Norway who claimed the throne on behalf of their leader, Earl Tostig, who incidentally was Harold's brother.

The Vikings were successfully repelled at the battle of Stamford Bridge but then a more potent threat materialised in Sussex. The Normans had landed in Sussex. Harold hurried south only stopping at Waltham to prostrate himself before the cross. Whilst he lay there on the ground the figure on the cross is said to have looked away. This was seen as an ill-omen, however the king was not told. In view of this the abbey insisted on sending two of their most trusted brethren, Osegod and Ailric, to accompany Harold to Hastings.

William, Duke of Normandy, having landed with his army had claimed the English throne. In the battle that followed Harold was despatched by that famous arrow in the eye.

Osegod and Ailric saw the king struck down. When the battle was over they began a painstaking search to find the body. This was very difficult as many of the dead had been stripped and mutilated. Harold's mistress Edith was summoned to Hastings to assist with identification. She recognised certain marks on one of the bodies as belonging to Harold. Immediately the monks asked the victorious William if they could remove the body to Waltham Abbey for burial. Initially William refused but eventually relented. Harold's remains were then collected and carried back to Waltham Abbey. Here Harold was buried with great honour and to this day a memorial stone marks his grave in the Abbey Gardens.

Waltham Abbey became rich from the pilgrims flocking to the *Shrine of the Holy Rood*. It remained wealthy until the time of Henry VIII. In 1540 the Abbey was dissolved and many of the buildings demolished as part of the king's break with Rome. As for the stone cross, it disappeared and has never been seen since.

SWEYN'S CASTLE

'*Et in hoc manerio fecit Suenue suum castellum*' was the old Latin translated as 'in this manor Sweyn made his castle'. This is written in the *Domesday Book* survey of 1086 and Rayleigh is the only castle in Essex that is mentioned.

Although King Harold had been killed and his forces comprehensively defeated by William the Conqueror at the Battle of Hastings there were still elements of Saxon resistance around. Following the victory William dismissed many of the Saxon Lords and confiscated their lands. He then appointed barons whom he considered loyal and authorised them to build castles at strategic locations around the country. These would serve as fortified strong points that could be defended and reinforced if serious trouble was to break out.

Robert Fitzwimarc was granted the 'Honour' of Rayleigh. Fitzwimarc was a Saxon but was also related to the Normans and some suspected that he gave assistance to the invaders at Hastings.

Rayleigh was in a good position midway between the rivers Crouch and Thames and the Mount afforded commanding views over the local Essex countryside. As an added bonus the estates included woodlands, vineyards, farm animals and the allegiance of all the people living in the area who were tied to the land.

Robert Fitzwimarc died a few years after the Battle of Hastings and it was left to his son Sweyn to construct the Castle. When finished, it was a substantial structure dominating the landscape. Sweyn's son and grandson in turn inherited the Castle and extended and strengthened it. With the land came honours and privileges. Sweyn's grandson Henry de Essex was the King's standard bearer.

King Henry II was actively engaged in suppressing the Welsh. On one of his forays with the King to Wales, Henry de Essex was accused of cowardice in the face of the enemy. Later he was challenged to 'trial by combat', which he lost and was apparently presumed dead. This was not the case as two monks discovered much to their shock when, on retrieving Henry's body, they found he was in fact alive.

Henry De Essex recovered and spent the rest of his life in a monastery in Reading. He never set foot in Rayleigh again. As a consequence of Henry's humiliation the De Essex family was disgraced and the Castle and estate at Rayleigh reverted back to the Kings charge.

The next castle owner by Royal Prerogative was Hubert de Burgh. De Burgh had distinguished himself fighting the French and rose to hold prominent positions during the reign of Henry III. The Rayleigh estate had grown to include the manor of Hadleigh. De Burgh concluded that Hadleigh would be a far superior position for a castle as there were excellent views over the Thames Estuary. With the enemy within vanquished he deemed there was more to fear from the enemy abroad who in any event would have come by sea.

The days of Sweyn's Castle as a major fortification were numbered. Richard II would later authorise Rayleigh people to remove its stone for other building work. This may have been a sop to appease the local population who were still seething from the ill-fated peasant's revolt (see pages 35 and 37). Soon the castle was no more and it reverted to farm lands and woods. A visitor today would find little or nothing in the way of fortifications. The Mount is now covered with trees and is a nature reserve administered by the National Trust.

THE DUKE OF BOULOGNE

Robert de Guernon fought with William the Conqueror
at the battle of Hastings he won victory with honour.
a cousin of the King, whose favour he gained,
as reward many English estates he obtained.

Robert de Guernon (or Robert Greno as he is referred to in the Domesday Book), Duke of Boulogne, would seem to have been related to William the Conqueror. He was one of William's commanders in the invasion and decisive victory over King Harold at Hastings in 1066. For his part in the battle William rewarded him with lands and estates in Essex. He became a major landowner in the county. One of his Manors was Ayot Montfitchet in the Anglo-Saxon settlement of Stansted. It was here that De Guernon built an impressive Norman motte and bailey fortress which became the headquarters of his barony. The large stone ringwork was surrounded by a wet ditch, or moat, with the bailey having strong ramparts and ditches to the north and east. The castle remained the family seat until the last of the male line, Richard de Montfitchet II, died around 1265. Almost nothing remains today but fragments of twelfth century stonework may be seen on the southern slopes.

On Robert's death his son, William, inherited the dukedom and dropped the name of de Guernon, adopting the name 'Montfitchet'. He gave the land for the foundation of the Cistercian Abbey at Stratford Longthorne, later also known as West Ham Abbey. This was largely destroyed during the dissolution (See page 47). Its remains now lie buried beneath the London Underground Jubilee line, some half a mile south of today's Stratford Broadway.

Of William's son, Gilbert de Montfitchet, little is known, but his son, Richard, held the office of Forester or Keeper of the Forests of Essex, with the custody of the King's house at Havering and other houses in the forest, given to him by King Henry II. In 1203, Richard died, leaving his son Richard II a minor. Richard II became a royal ward of King John and was placed in the care of Roger de Lacey, Constable of Chester. As soon as he became of age, even though he had previously fought with the king in France, he joined the baronial opposition which led to the Magna Carta, incurring the wrath of King John. Following the Runnymede agreement King John reneged on the promises he had made and set about attacking the baronial rebels, beginning in Essex with Richard de Montfitchet.

King John's forces attacked Montfitchet castle in December 1215. There are conflicting accounts as to what happened but Richard was absent at the time and escaped with his life. However his stronghold was destroyed. The ruins of the castle were subsequently pillaged by local people for anything of value, even the very stone.

Mountfitchet Castle

After two years of war and King John's death, Richard de Montfitchet, along with all the other rebel barons, was returned to royal favour by the new King, Henry III. All the Montfitchet estates were restored to him. Henry also granted Richard a Tuesday market at West Ham as well as an annual fair on the 19th to 22nd of July. Both of these were discontinued in the late eighteenth century.

Though married at least twice, Richard died in 1267 aged around 70 without issue. The vast manor of Ayot Montfitchet, or Ayot St Peter as it was also known, was inherited by his three sisters, Margery, Avelina and Phillippa. None of them showed any interest in the castle at Stansted Montfitchet and it remained in ruins. The site became overgrown and lay forgotten for over seven hundred years until its reconstruction in 1984 as a tourist attraction.

Built on the original site the reconstruction depicts the wooden palisaded motte and bailey castle of the eleventh century. Occupying a commanding position overlooking the Stort valley, it has throughout history been strategically important. Prior to the Norman invasion and the arrival of Robert de Guernon it had been an Iron Age hill fort, a Roman signals fort and later a Saxon and Viking settlement. Now it is a unique time capsule and visitors may step back in history to wander through the Norman village enclosed within.

MAGNA CARTA

"No free man shall be seized or imprisoned", clause 39 began
or stripped of his rights or possessions, or outlawed", it ran

"or exiled, except by the lawful judgment of his equals" to hand,
"and only deprived of his standing by the law of the land"

On 15th June 1215 what was to become known as Magna Carta was sealed by King John at Runnymede, on land owned by Richard de Montfitchet. The Magna Carta or Great Charter was essentially a peace treaty between the King of England and the nobility. It had come about due to widespread dissatisfaction with the king's rule. During the course of his 14 year reign King John had bankrupted the country in pursuit of his territorial claims in France. As a consequence he had imposed a series of harsh taxes to refill the treasury. Yet, it was not just financial matters that made King John so despised by his subjects. Baronial lands could be confiscated on the whim of the king and even a minor disagreement could lead to exile. Suspicion also lingered over King John's role in the mysterious disappearance in a French prison of his rival contender to the throne, his nephew prince Arthur. Even some of his loyal supporters saw him at times as cruel and tyrannical. The resentment of the people was fuelled by John's reliance on an army of foreign mercenaries to enforce his rule during the baron's war.

As opposition to the king grew, Robert Fitzwalter, the Lord of Dunmow, and self-styled *Marshal of the Army of God and the Holy Church*, stepped forward to lead a powerful group of rebels charged with bringing the 'Magna Carta' to fruition. After the sealing at Runneymede, Fitzwalter headed a council of twenty five barons whose role was to enforce the charter's terms. With him were three other Essex men, Richard de Montfitchet, Geoffrey de Mandeville of Pleshey and Robert de Vere of Castle Hedingham. They were joined by William de Lanvallei, the Governor of Colchester Castle, whose baronial seat was in Hertfordshire, Roger and Hugh Bigod of Framlingham Castle in neighbouring Suffolk and John FitzRobert, of Warkworth Castle (in Northumberland) who had extensive landholdings around Saffron Walden.

The Magna Carta's overriding principle was that the monarch was not above the law and could only act in accordance with the legal principles laid down in it. However, within days King John claimed that he had agreed only under duress; his subsequent actions demonstrated that he had no intention of honouring it anyway. By September 1215 the Magna Carta had been effectively torn up and England was in a state of war. The king mustered those still loyal to him (a large part of whom were foreign mercenaries) and set about bringing the rebels to heel. The Pope, (Innocent III) sided with King John and excommunicated all the rebels. He viewed the barons' actions as a direct assault upon the divine right of the king to rule. In August 1215, he issued a papal bull annulling the charter.

The barons, for their part, sought help from King Philip of France. They called on his son Prince Louis, who also had a claim to the English throne, to come to England and take the crown. War began in earnest in October 1215 when King John attacked Rochester castle in Kent. He then divided his forces taking one half of his army north, while the remainder of his mercenaries moved into Essex and East Anglia creating havoc and fear as they went. In quick succession Montfitchet and Pleshey Castles were taken and within four months Framlingham, Colchester and Hedingham Castles also capitulated.

In May 1216 Prince Louis arrived in England to support the barons and claim the crown and the balance swung in favour of the rebels. King John, retreating northwards, became ill and died of dysentery at Newark in October 1216. The situation then dramatically changed. The new English king, Henry III, reissued a revised Magna Carta which served to turn the tables on Prince Louis and the rebels. Following a series of military defeats Louis renounced his claim and returned to France in September 1217.

After swearing loyalty to the new king all the rebel barons were returned to favour and regained their lands. It is remarkable that none of the barons were killed 'in action' during two years of warfare. The only one to die prematurely was Geoffrey de Mandeville who was killed accidentally by one of his allies in a jousting tournament.

The ultimate triumph for Robert Fitzwalter, the leader of the rebel barons, was to witness the 1225 re-confirmation of the Magna Cart before the king and Grand Council in Westminster.

The charter that King John sealed at Runnymede on 15th June 1215 lies at the root of the British constitution. It was the beginning of all the freedoms that the British people were to gain over the next eight hundred years. However, despite the Magna Carta with its 63 clauses being written in 1215, today the United Kingdom still has no written constitution.

HADLEIGH CASTLE

Hadleigh Castle built on clay, Was Hubert's folly locals say.
T'will tumble down from its base, and like de Burgh fall from grace.

Hadleigh Castle is over 750 years old. The castle has seen many comings and goings and several of the characters that crop up in this book have visited it. Quite a few have even owned it! The original licence to build was granted to Hubert de Burgh, Earl of Kent and Chief Judicial Officer to King John.

The castle is now a shadow of its former self. In the great medieval scheme of things it replaced the castle at Rayleigh. The site was considered ideal as it offered magnificent views across the Thames estuary from where any threatened seaborne invasion might come. However, in spite of great effort and expense, the castle's completion simply offered nothing more than a splendid view from the ramparts. It was useless as a deterrent as shot from the primitive artillery of the day could never hit ships entering the Thames. The castle served no strategic purpose as invaders could easily pass it, therefore leaving the defenders wondering what to do next. Royalty were little inclined to visit as the journey to Hadleigh from London was difficult both by land and water.

De Burgh was one of the few loyalists supporting the king in his battles with the barons over the Magna Carta. After John's death Henry III kept De Burgh as his Chief Minister but serious plotting by disgruntled barons eventually secured his dismissal, arrest and imprisonment. Though later pardoned, he never regained high office.

Over time numerous renovations were undertaken and the castle suffered from its fair share of shoddy builders. Successive kings spent small fortunes then each in turn lost interest. During the 100 years war with France, King Edward III authorised a complete rebuild and it is said he even lodged there to check up on the workmen. A later illustrious occupant was Aubrey de Vere, the 10th Earl of Oxford. He held the post of Constable of the Castle and gave shelter to plotters trying to restore Richard II to the throne after he was deposed (see Silence of Pleshey Castle page 38). De Vere allegedly died at the castle on 23rd April 1400, St George's day, and is buried in the Hadleigh area.

The long war with France came to an end in the 15th century and the castle went through a succession of owners. There is no record of it ever being attacked. The castle's main enemies were the sea, the salty air and the unstable ground on which it was built.

The final demise of the castle began in the time of Henry VIII. He showed no interest other than passing the castle and surrounding land off on three of his wives. However there is no record of any of them staying there. The nine year old Edward VI inherited the Castle from his father. He was a sickly child and died at the age of 15. During his short reign the castle was abandoned and fast became a ruin. However in 1551 Edward was persuaded to sell it to Lord, later Baron, Richard Riche of Leez Priory.

Riche, perhaps the original 'Essex wide boy', saw a business opportunity and an asset to be stripped. He obtained Hadleigh Castle for £700. Much of the castle was quickly demolished, with the stone and fittings sold or carted off to one of the many other building projects Lord Riche had in hand at the time. What remained of the castle deteriorated over time due to regular landslips and the ruins still standing began to disappear under vegetation. In 1814 the landscape painter John Constable, while visiting his uncle in Leigh-on-Sea, made a drawing of the castle followed by ten oil sketches, known as his 'six footers', as preparation for a single painting. The final painting, finished in 1829, is now in the 'Yale Center for British Art' in America. One of the sketches, a masterpiece in its own right, hangs in the Tate Gallery in London.

The Salvation Army acquired the ruins in 1891, together with much of the surrounding land, when its farm colony was created. After the Second World War the Castle site was given to the Ministry of Works.

Hadleigh Castle is now owned by English Heritage. Classed as a scheduled monument, with a grade 1 listing, it is open to the public with free entry. In August 2012, part of Hadleigh Farm adjacent to the castle was used as the venue for the 2012 Olympic two day Mountain Biking event.

St GEORGE and the DRAGON

The Essex village of Wormingford lies just south of the River Stour, the county border with Suffolk, about nine miles north-west of Colchester. In the centre of Wormingford, the village sign supports a weather vane capped by a metal sculpture of a knight on horseback lancing a dragon-like creature. A little further on, in Church Lane, the 12th century St Andrews' Church stands above the middle reaches of the River Stour. Just below, across the river, is Smallbridge Hall, where Sir William Waldegrave entertained Elizabeth I. On the horizon is Arger Fen nature reserve and the hill upon which Edmund was crowned King of East Anglia on Christmas Day, 856. Within the church, the stained glass east window of the north aisle also depicts a mounted knight slaying a dragon, although in this case, more graphically, as two legs of a maiden are seen protruding from the dragon's jaws. It has given Essex and Wormingford its very own version of the St. George and the Dragon story.

The above is certainly true but how the dragon story came about is the subject of various theories. The most credible appears to be that the 'dragon' was a crocodile which was brought back by King Richard I on his return from the crusades and placed in a strong cage at the Tower of London. (A menagerie existed at the Tower from 1210 until 1832 when the animals were removed to London Zoo). The creature then escaped and disappeared without trace. Despite substantial rewards being offered, the 'dragon' made its way through the marshlands of Essex to the River Stour, terrorising people and devouring several sheep on its journey.

From the Stour the creature emerged into the town of Sudbury where it created widespread panic among the inhabitants. Witnesses reported to have seen with their own eyes, "an enormous monster emerging from the water and breathing fire in the general direction of anything that moved". Some townsmen gallantly took up arms to confront the strange creature but their arrows merely bounced off its tough skin. Nevertheless the creature retreated to the river and disappeared. Nothing remotely resembling such a monster had ever been seen before and the consensus was that it was a dragon containing the spirit of the devil. Word rapidly spread throughout the surrounding countryside and fearful villagers banded together to defend themselves. The 'dragon's' next reported appearance was further downstream on the Stour, in Bures, where a shepherd and most of his flock of sheep were said to have been killed.

Numerous attempts were made by locals to slay the 'dragon', all unsuccessful, as their arrows and stones again simply bounced of the 'dragon's' scaly skin. Nevertheless the 'dragon' withdrew and this time disappeared into the waters of Wormingford Mere never to be seen again.

Yet an elaborate 500 word legend that hangs on the wall in Wormingford Church, by the stained glass window, suggests that the 'dragon' re-emerged and began to ravage the locality around Wormingford. Rumour spread among the villagers that the creature could only be pacified with sacrificial virgins. However the supply of virgins in 'Withermundford', as Wormingford was originally called, soon ran out and the 'dragon' could no longer be tamed. In desperation the villagers called for the dashing knight, Sir George of Layer de la Haye, son of the Earl of Boulogne, to slay the beast.

The 'dashing' knight duly heeded the villagers' request and set about his mission. There then followed a somewhat anti-climactic ending to the story. Rather than telling tales of derring-do, a fight of life and death with a ferocious fire breathing creature and rescuing a maiden or two from the jaws of death, Sir George simply said; "'I chased the dragon and slew it. It really put up a poor fight".

So Essex had its very own St. George and seemingly its very own dragon although in all probability the dragon was a crocodile suffering from bad breath rather than having any fire eating capabilities.

Nevertheless just across the River Stour at Wissingham (or Wiston) the 11th century, grade 1 listed, Norman Church of St. Mary the Virgin has a 15th century wall painting of a fire eating dragon too!

DOG OF WAR

'Giovanni Acuto' the Italians called him.
Learned his trade with The Black Prince in France.
Thought by Chaucer 'a gentle and courteous man',
The 'Diabolical Englishman' led Italy a dance.

Sir John Hawkwood was, if not the original, then certainly the most famous, and most feared, soldier of fortune in late Middle Age Italy. Born about 1320 in Sible Hedingham, he was the second of three sons of a tanner and minor landowner.

The Hundred Years War with France was a magnet that attracted many young men to seek fame and fortune, John Hawkwood was one of them. He learned his trade fighting with the Black Prince at Poitiers. He became a brilliant tactician and commander who looked after his men and was knighted for his loyalty to the King.

The temporary peace after the treaty of Brétigny meant Hawkwood was left at a loose end. All he knew was war and it was as much about looting as about winning. Being the younger son he had nothing to go back to in England. With thousands of other mercenaries in the same position, he drifted south through France.

Having seen how easy it was to extract money from poorly defended villages, in return for protection organised groups of mercenaries laid siege to the town of Pont-Saint-Esprit. Having decimated the town they turned to nearby Avignon, the seat of the Pope. Hawkwood's career as a 'Condottiere,' in modern terms 'gun for hire,' began here. Pope Innocent VI, fearing an all out attack, paid the leaders, one of them Hawkwood, to take their mercenaries and go to Italy.

Chaucer, who had met Hawkwood, wrote in his Prologue to the Canterbury Tales of *a verray, parfit gentil knyght* who *loved chivalrie, trouthe and honour, fredom and curtesie.* These were not characteristics that many in Italy would recognise in the man they would come to know as Giovanni Acuto, the *Diabolical Englishman.*

Many Italian city-states such as Milan, Florence, Pisa and Sienna were vying with each other for supremacy, all fearing attack in one form or another. It was here in northern Italy that Hawkwood's 'White Company' became the most efficient, ruthless and feared force ever. They would work to contracts, negotiated by Hawkwood, for the highest bidder. After putting whole towns under occupation they would purposely destroy harvests to ensure starvation if that was what their paymasters wanted. Terror was their main weapon but if there was no money forthcoming they would burn everything.

In 1377 at Cesena, near Rimini, Hawkwood's mercenaries cold bloodedly murdered as many as 5,000 inhabitants in a savagely organised act of reprisal on the orders of Pope Gregory. The same year, at the age of 57, Hawkwood married the seventeen year old Donnina, daughter of Bernabo Visconti the ruthless ruler of Milan. The alliance with Milan did not last since there was no loyalty from the mercenaries if a better offer came along. And a better offer did come, from Florence. He had fought against the Florentines in the past, now he was hired to protect them and to attack their enemies.

Hawkwood's cold and calculating ruthlessness earned him the title of the *Diabolical Englishman* yet he became a hero in Florence. Giovanni Acuto (Acuto was the nearest the Italians could get to saying Hawkwood) was honoured by the grateful city. His image, in a fresco by Paulo Uccello, adorns the east nave of Florence Cathedral.

He died in 1394 and his remains were transferred to his hometown of Sible Hedingham for burial.

ONE NIGHT IN BOXTED

King Edward III had come to nearby Colchester's estate
And official records show he entered by the Balkerne gate.
Yet he left almost immediately so what was going on?
Local dignitaries waited patiently, but the King had gone.

Edward III, King of England, spent most of his reign fighting the French during the course of the 100 years war. When not at war he promoted English as the national language and oversaw reforms to the legal system. In 1354 there was a truce between the English and the French. When the weather was better and the days longer, the king travelled around the country with his mobile court, the Chancery, trying to resolve some of the more intractable local disputes.

The town of Colchester had been involved in a long dispute with Lionel de Bradenhan, the Lord of Langenhoe Manor. Bradenhan was described as an Essex gentleman but his actions were more like a tyrant. His men had besieged the town and ambushed officials attempting to travel in or out. He demanded ransom for those caught. He had plundered the oyster beds on the river Colne and blocked local water-courses. Furthermore he broke open the town gaol and interfered with the duties of the local coroner. He was certainly one reason for the King Edward to come to Colchester.

Although the date cannot be confirmed it was probably at Michaelmas (29th September 1354). It is known that the 'Law Hundred' - or Court of the Borough - was usually held on this day. Edward would probably have travelled from London, stopping overnight at the Royal Manor at Writtle, before moving on to Colchester. With the king expected all the town dignitaries were in attendance. Waiting close to the Balkerne Gate a ceremonial guard was lined up. Suitable lodging would have been arranged and a sumptuous feast prepared. Onlookers jostled for the best position to see the king. Midday arrived and suddenly there was a great commotion. The king was seen entering through the Balkerne Gate. However his face was not visible through the phalanx of bodyguards, soldiers and court officials. The king appeared to come closer to the reception committee but then vanished. That was it! The civic leaders of Colchester waited and waited. Where was the king? Then word came that the king was not coming and had never intended to come to Colchester in the first place so the court should proceed without him.

Legend has it that Edward came to Colchester on the date in question but for a completely different motive. He had absolutely no intention of presiding over the law hundred. Officers of the King's Court were sent into Colchester, creating confusion.

Edward himself had gone straight from Writtle to Boxted Hall, arriving late afternoon accompanied only by his personal retinue. Boxted Hall was the family home of Peter de Boxted, Sheriff of Essex.

Peter's duties meant regular absences from his estate on the king's business sometimes accompanied by his wife, Lady Sybil. At the time of their marriage Sybil, a vivacious, attractive girl who moved well in aristocratic circles, was young enough to be Peter's granddaughter. On one of their visits to the Royal Court she was 'noticed' by the king.

It so happened at Michaelmas, 29th September 1354, Peter de Boxted was away on official business; Lady Sybil was at home alone in Boxted Hall, and the King was certainly 'missing' from his duties in Colchester. Sybil may have got her man for one night in Boxted but Colchester's leading citizens had definitely been stood up!

King Edward III

THREE DAYS THAT SHOOK THE KINGDOM

Thomas Brampton, King Richard's tax collector
Empowered to deal harshly with any objector.
Entered Brentwood with his clerks in tow,
Any waiver requests would be met with a firm NO!

In May 1381 England was recovering from the 'Black Death', a plague that killed between one third and half of the population. At the same time the nation was embroiled with its '100 years' war with France. The war was not going well and was expensive. The majority of the army overseas had not been paid for months. The decline in population had substantially reduced tax revenues and put a severe strain on the feudal system that effectively obliged labourers to work for a specific manorial Lord in perpetuity. There was now a labour shortage and in many cases men simply left their manors to find work elsewhere for better wages and conditions, even though this was against laws enacted to control labour.

Parliament was determined to raise money. Five years earlier it had introduced the first poll tax. This head tax had applied to almost everyone over the age of 14. A second poll tax was levied in 1379 and, in 1380, a third, charging one shilling, or 3 groats (5p), on all people over the age of 16. It was hoped that the richer elements in society would help the poor; piously expressed at the time as 'the strong might aid the weak'. This was the case in some areas but in many places the tax was a heavy burden.

This latest tax managed to antagonise nearly everyone and led to widespread evasion. Official population figures for Essex in 1381 showed a dramatic decrease in population of between 35 – 40% from the previously recorded figure. This downward adjustment of the population figures was achieved with the connivance of local civic leaders who simply understated the local population on their returns. Parliament became suspicious and sent commissioners to check on the accuracy of the numbers of people liable to pay the tax.

On 30th May 1381, John Bampton, an Essex JP and the Estate Steward of Barking Abbey, was sent to Brentwood accompanied by Sir John Gilsburgh MP, the Speaker of the House of Commons, to conduct enquiries into the Barstable Hundred. John Bampton was notoriously corrupt. During his career he had acquired several properties in Essex by dubious means. Sir John Gilsburgh also owned many properties in Essex including a large estate and Manor House at Wennington, close to Aveley.

He was also an unashamed champion of the war with France and had campaigned energetically in Parliament for additional funds to billet the English army in Brittany during the winter. The commissioners set up court close to the Thomas à Becket Chapel* in Brentwood. On being told by the leader of those summoned, Thomas Baker, that not a penny more would be paid, they ordered his arrest. This resulted in a riot and the commissioners, with their entourage, fled for their lives back to London.

Three days later, on Whit Sunday 2nd June, a High Court Judge, Sir Robert Belknap, arrived with the task of restoring order and resuming the enquiry. He was given strict orders to seek out and punish the rioters. However, the Essex men were well prepared. During the intervening three days messengers had galloped all over Essex and what is now East London, calling for resistance at Brentwood. The mob had now grown to thousands and the Judge's 'hard man' approach only inflamed them further. Riot again ensued. Belknap was manhandled then stripped and made to swear an oath on the bible. He was lucky to escape with his life. Three of his clerks were not so fortunate. They were seized and beheaded, as were some local jurors accused of collaborating. Their heads were put on poles for all to see. All the court records were then burnt in a huge bonfire. The incident was a catalyst that sparked the 'Peasants' or 'Great Revolt' in Essex.

Almost immediately attacks took place all over the county, especially on those associated with Parliament. As always, criminals and other malcontents used the opportunity to loot and burn and settle scores. The Essex rebels joined with those of Kent, who were led by Wat Tyler, and laid siege to London. The government of Richard II was nearly toppled after the rebels captured the Tower of London, destroyed the Savoy palace, home of John of Gaunt, and in the process killed the Chancellor, the Chief Justice and The Treasurer.

Two weeks after it all began on 15th June, Richard II confronted the rebels at Smithfield. Their leader Wat Tyler, who was worse the wear for drink whilst attempting to speak with the King, died after skirmishing with William Walworth, the Mayor of London. The young King Richard, only 14 years old, faced the crowd and won them over with promises of fair treatment and claims on their loyalty. The Revolt was effectively over. Wat Tyler is remembered today as a hero of the people and is commemorated in Pitsea by the 'Wat Tyler Country Park'.

The remains of Thomas à Becket Chapel are in Brentwood High Street. It was a popular stopping point for pilgrims travelling south on their way to Canterbury in the middle ages.

RETRIBUTION

Essex was where 'The whole madness first sprang'
So it was only natural the ringleaders would hang.
The King lodged at Writtle where his edicts flowed
For seven days, in a torrent that never slowed.

Following the death of Wat Tyler, and the peaceful dispersal of his followers at Smithfield, King Richard II moved swiftly to impose his authority. Elements of the rebellion were still active in the country. In Essex a sizeable rebel group, that had massed near Billericay, was confronted and defeated by forces loyal to the king.

As the countryside was secured the royal court moved from London to Havering and on to Chelmsford. From 1st July until 6th July 1381 the King lodged in the Royal Palace* at Writtle. For seven days Writtle became the seat of Government. Edicts and proclamations were produced almost non-stop and messengers carried them to all corners of the kingdom. Their substance was that the rebellion was over and the only lawful authority was the king or his appointees. Furthermore, any promises made to the rebels earlier were withdrawn as they had been made 'under duress'. To quash any hopes that lingered of new found freedoms Richard II stated *Villeins ye are still and villeins ye shall remain.* **

Following the death of the Chief Justice Sir John Cavendish, killed by the rebels, the king appointed Sir Robert Tresilian. He set up court in Chelmsford with the purpose of bringing the instigators of the revolt to justice. Delegations of 'rebels' came to Chelmsford begging for mercy.

Tresilian promised to spare their lives if the ringleaders were named. Over 145 rebel leaders were identified. No mercy was shown to those who were caught. After a short trial they were executed and their property confiscated. Included in these was Thomas Baker from Fobbing. Although the status quo returned, there was no doubt the rebellion had rocked the establishment to its core. The Chancellor, the Chief Justice and the Treasurer had been killed. Several Royal lodges and 'Official' buildings had been looted then burned and most of the local records had been destroyed along with them. In a final twist Parliament declared a general amnesty to all rebels still at large on 14th December 1381.

Formerly King John's Palace and now the site of Writtle College.

**The word *Villien* is derived from the French or Latin villanus, meaning serf or peasant, someone who is tied to the land and manor.*

THE SILENCE OF PLESHEY CASTLE

Ghosts of long dead Dukes and Earls
Reflect on dark deeds of jealous Kings
Atop the mound; all that remains,
Of Pleshey's once resplendent halls.

The village of Pleshey lies in the parish of High Easter, between Chelmsford and Dunmow. It was given to Geoffrey de Mandeville by William the Conqueror as a reward for his support at the battle of Hastings. As High Constable of England he became one of the most powerful men in Essex with Pleshey Castle as his family seat. The castle would have been a typical Norman earthwork, motte and bailey with wooden palisades and tower and by the end of the twelfth century it was the home of Geoffrey's grandson, Geoffrey III, Earl of Essex.

By the 14th century the castle had passed, through inheritance, to Eleanor de Bohun. When she married Thomas of Woodstock, Duke of Gloucester and the youngest son of Edward III, the castle became their home. Gloucester was also uncle to, and one of the guardians of, the young King Richard II. On reaching maturity Richard tired of the interference of his guardians, particularly Gloucester. And so began, in 1397, one of the most infamous events in the history of Pleshey.

King Richard, while staying at his house in Havering-Atte-Bower, now part of Romford, paid an allegedly friendly, but unexpected, visit to his uncle at Pleshey. Welcomed, he dined there and then persuaded

Gloucester to accompany him to London for a meeting the next day with his other uncles, York and Lancaster. They set off and on reaching Stratford the king rode on ahead leaving his uncle to be ambushed by the Earl Marshal and a troop of men. Gloucester was arrested 'in the king's name,' taken to the Thames and put aboard a ship bound for Calais. He was declared a traitor and all his lands were confiscated by the crown. When requests for his return to face trial were sent to Calais the reply came back that Gloucester had died in prison. How he died was never disclosed but an inquisition set up after the accession of King Henry IV found, "…that he had been fraudulently and wickedly smothered, by the king's orders at Calais".

This episode in the life of Pleshey is immortalised by William Shakespeare in his play, Richard the Second, where he uses it as the trigger for Henry (Bolingbroke) to depose Richard and seize the crown.

The RISE and FALL of BARKING ABBEY

Henry V died leaving widow Catherine
And baby son Henry to reign as king.
Owen Tudor then made Catherine his wife
Of lowly rank he was the love of her life.

When Henry V died in 1422 he left a young widow, Catherine de Valois, and a nine year old son who became King Henry VI. Catherine, still a young woman, later secretly married and had four children with Owen Tudor, a commoner. When their secret became known the young king's guardians were furious. The liaison and children was one thing but legal marriage could not be tolerated. Owen Tudor fled to refuge in Wales; Catherine to sanctuary in Bermondsey Abbey. The children, at the behest of their half brother the King, were sent to Barking Abbey where they were educated as royalty. One of the children, Edmund, was later created earl of Richmond and married Margaret Beaufort. Their only son Henry, was to became the first Tudor King, Henry VII.

The Abbey had a long association with royalty. Founded in 666 by Erkenwald for his sister Ethelburga, it was endowed with land and property by many East Saxon Princes. Destroyed by Vikings in 870, it was rebuilt a hundred years later by Edward the Elder as a royal foundation, with the appointment of each abbess being the prerogative of the king. Its importance grew such that William the Conqueror, at the end of 1066, established his court there while the Tower of London was being built. Over the next 300 years the abbey was enlarged and extended to become one of the most impressive religious buildings in England.

Abbesses of Barking included queens and princesses and would hold precedence over all other abbesses. At its peak the abbey was one of the biggest land owners in the south of England. It had extensive property holdings throughout Essex including large estates around Colchester, Harlow, Benfleet, Stansted and Brentwood. It was the third wealthiest nunnery in the country and enjoyed a huge annual net income.

Dorothy Barley was the Abbess in place when Henry VIII dissolved England's monasteries (see page 47). During some dissolutions monasteries could be seized by unscrupulous agents of the king, the occupants summarily evicted, the buildings looted, and all records burnt. Abbess Barley however was very well connected. She was a friend of Sir William Petre, a lawyer who had taken possession of the abbey. She was godmother to Petre's daughter and his sister was one of her nuns.

Petre received the deed of surrender of the abbey, and all its possessions, from Barley on 14th November 1539. In return she received a generous pension and was ensured that her nuns would be treated well. (During this transaction Petrie acquired the Abbey's manor of Ingatestone where his decendants live to this day.)

A year after Dorothy Barley departed, demolition of the abbey buildings began in earnest and carried on for 18 months. The road to Creekmouth was repaired with abbey stone and much of the remainder was shipped down the Thames for building the king's new house at Dartford.

For the next four hundred years the site was virtually a quarry. After excavations of the original site in 1910 all that remains of Barking Abbey today is the Curfew Tower or Fire Bell Gate which stands alongside the surviving St Margaret's Parish Church. The footprint of the abbey has been preserved as an open space and stretches from old Barking Town Hall to the abbey retail park on the banks of the River Roding. Since 1975 it has been a conservation area. However, with the industrial revolution and the steady expansion of London, new factories, warehouses, offices and, later, retail outlets and housing sprang up along the banks of the River Roding encroaching onto the former abbey lands. It is quite possible that if the conservation order had not been made in 1975 the remaining site would have disappeared too.

THE DUNMOW FLITCH

You shall swear by the Custom of our Confession
That you never made any Nuptial Transgression
For this is our Custom at Dunmow well known
Though the sport be ours, the bacon's your own.

Over nine hundred years ago Reginald Fitzwalter and his wife decided that their marriage lasting a year and a day without regrets was deserving of recognition. Disguising themselves in humble clothing they approached the Augustinian Prior to bless their union. Afterwards Fitzwalter revealed his identity as Lord of the Manor and in gratitude gave the priory some land. The gift was conditional on a flitch, or side, of bacon being awarded annually to a couple who could demonstrate a similar devotion. This as legend would have it is how, in 1104, the 'Dunmow Flitch' was born.

The modern trials, held every leap year, take place in Great Dunmow in a court with a presiding judge. Counsel represents the claimants who have been married for a year and a day. Opposing counsel appears for the donors of the Flitch of Bacon. A jury of six maidens and six bachelors has to be persuaded. A clerk records the proceedings with an usher keeping order.

Successful couples are carried shoulder high in the ancient Flitch Chair to the Market Place where they take the oath kneeling on pointed stones. The unsuccessful couples walk behind and receive a consolation prize of gammon.

The Dunmow Flitch trials were a widely known tradition in the fourteenth century since they are mentioned by William Langland in his book, 'The Vision of Piers Plowman', in 1362. The first recorded winner of a flitch though was Richard Wright of Norwich in 1445.

After the dissolution of the monasteries by Henry VIII the custom seems to have lapsed until the Lord of the Manor briefly revived it in the eighteenth century. Thomas Shakeshaft and his wife, who won the flitch in 1751, immediately cut it up and sold it piecemeal to the crowd. The Lord of the Manor, perhaps understandably distressed by this, lost interest and the ceremony lapsed again.

The trials were revived again around 1855 as a civic event, mainly through the efforts of Harrison Ainsworth* who, in 1854, wrote a very popular book entitled, *The Flitch of Bacon or The Custom of Dunmow.*

In this Ainsworth tells of a young man trying to win the 'Flitch' by marrying a succession of wives in order to find a perfect one.

Since then the event has only been interrupted by the two wars, although since World War Two the annual event has given way to leap year trials mentioned at the beginning of this chapter.

*In 1834 Harrison Ainsworth also wrote 'Rookwood' which was responsible for most of the myth surrounding Dick Turpin. (See page 74, Stand and Deliver)

LOYAL SUBJECT HENRY MARNEY

On Bosworth's bloody field Henry Marney made his name.
Richard III had lost the crown to which Henry VII now laid claim.

The Marneys had lived in Layer Marney for nearly three hundred years before Henry was born in 1447. They had come to England in the wake of William the Conqueror. By 1414 the family had a certain status in the county since Henry's grandfather William had become Sheriff of Essex.

Henry Marney was a loyal supporter of Henry Tudor in the Wars of the Roses. He fought at the battles of Stoke and Bosworth Field and was knighted after the resounding defeat of Perkin Warbeck and his Cornish rebels at Blackheath in 1497.

The Wars of the Roses were effectively ended at Bosworth. Richard III had been killed, his forces routed and Henry Tudor was proclaimed king in the field. On being crowned, Henry VII did not forget his supporters. Henry Marney was appointed to the Privy Council. He was a friend, confidante and guide to the king and remained a Privy Councillor when the king died, serving his son, Henry VIII. Under Henry VIII, Marney gained many honours and was eventually created Lord Marney.

Marney planned to build a grand house at Layer Marney. Modelled upon Wolsey's Hampton Court Palace, it was to be even more magnificent. Unfortunately he died in 1523 leaving his son, Lord Marney II, to complete the building. He also died suddenly two years later, leaving a partly rebuilt Church of St Mary the Virgin, a stable block, the front side of the Courtyard Palace and the main house not yet started. Provision in both their wills allowed for the church to be completed. The finished church contains the tombs of father and son, the first and last Lords Marney.

John Marney left two daughters who sold the estate in 1533 to Sir Brian Tuke, High Sheriff of Essex. His son George added the spectacular eight storey, four turreted gatehouse – now at eighty feet the tallest Tudor gatehouse in the country. Henry Marney's dream house was never built and the building became known as Layer Marney Tower. The estate then passed through many hands and had been almost continuously occupied for generations. It was considerably damaged in the Great Earthquake of 1884, (see page 131) though it was repaired soon afterwards.

In 1959 the house came into the possession of the Charrington family who have been in residence since then.

TO MARRY A KING

Rochford 100 golf course, so serene.
The thwack! Of golf balls on the green.

Rochford has two visible reminders of the town's part in the saga of the country's most married king: 'The Anne Boleyn' pub, named after Rochford's most famous daughter, and 'Rochford Hundred Golf Club', which occupies her one time family home, Rochford Hall.

The Manor of Rochford has passed through many hands since its 12th century association with the De Rochford family. Acquired by Thomas Boleyn in the early fifteen hundreds, it became the Boleyn family home in 1525 when he was given the title Viscount Rochford. Some said this was because his eldest daughter Mary had been Henry VIII's mistress.

Thomas had three children, George, Mary and Anne - probably all born at the family seat, Blickling Hall in Norfolk, between 1499 and 1507. The Boleyns' fortunes took a setback when Henry tired of Mary but looked up when he met sister Anne and fell madly in love. The king often hunted in the forests around Rochford and was said to have visited Anne at Rochford Hall. However there are no records to actually confirm that Anne ever stayed in Rochford. Thomas Boleyn, hoping to increase his prestige and power at court, feverishly encouraged the match. Settling for nothing less than marriage, Anne became queen. She was pregnant when they married in 1533 and in September gave birth to the future Queen Elizabeth.

However, she had many enemies at court and politically motivated plots and intrigues against her abounded. Yet, it was her inability to produce a son and heir that led to her downfall. In time Henry's attentions wandered and when Jane Seymour came on the scene, Anne had to go. On trumped up charges she was accused of treason and adultery with her brother George among others. Unable to help, Thomas Boleyn was forced to preside over the trial of five other men accused with Anne and George. Thomas condemned them all but the king excused him from being involved in the trial of his children. Anne and George were found guilty and Thomas Boleyn had to witness their executions.

Mary had earlier been the king's mistress whilst married to Sir William Carey. She had two children, Henry and Catherine - there was speculation, never substantiated, that their father was Henry VIII. She inherited the estate on her father's death. In 1552 her son sold Rochford Hall to Lord Richard Riche.

TYNDALE'S FRIEND

At dead of night standing at the quayside
Thomas Poyntz awaited the incoming tide

William Tyndale was ordained as a priest in 1521. A talented scholar, his ambition was to translate the Latin Bible into English so that people could read it for themselves. They would not then have to accept whatever the clergy told them. This was strictly forbidden in Henry VIII's England. Church leaders such as Cardinal Wolsey, and later Thomas More, vigorously enforced the law.

Tyndale began translating the New Testament but was forced to flee England to Germany where he eventually completed it. By 1526 copies were being read in England, albeit behind closed doors. King Henry's spies were everywhere and although Tyndale was still abroad he had to be very careful. In 1534, he decided to move to Antwerp where he thought he could live safely.

There were many 'English Houses' in Antwerp. Thomas Poyntz, an Essex merchant from North Ockendon, ran one of them. Poyntz was sympathetic to reform and welcomed Tyndale to his house. It was here that Tyndale continued his work, translating and publishing the complete English Bible. They were printed by the thousand.

There was considerable trade between England and Antwerp. Bibles could be shipped relatively easily, hidden in bales of cloth, in barrels or disguised as boxes of legal goods. It was a highly risky business since the east coast ports of England were watched continuously. Merchants such as Poyntz, keen supporters of church reformation, had to be very careful. Shipments were made at the dead of night and often to little known places like Purfleet. The contraband then had to be dispersed which was also extremely dangerous. Seen as a heretic by the church, and not only in England, Tyndale had many enemies. One of these, Henry Phillips, an agent posing as a friend, betrayed him to the authorities. He was arrested and imprisoned in Vilvoorde Castle in what is now Belgium. The strenuous activities of Poyntz and his family in petitioning Thomas Cromwell and Henry VIII for Tyndale's release and extradition all failed. In 1536, after being incarcerated for 18 months, Tyndale was taken to the Market Square, tied to a stake and then strangled. His body was then burnt. Thomas Poyntz, also branded as a heretic by Henry Phillips, was put under house arrest in Antwerp but managed to escape to England.

Despite the fact that John Poyntz, his elder brother, was a member of the household of Queen Catherine of Aragon, and had been at 'The Field of the Cloth of Gold' with Henry VIII, Thomas' life was in ruins on his return. As a known heretic he was under surveillance by Henry's spies and his continued involvement in the spreading of the new bible meant life was very difficult.

Thomas may have felt vindicated when, two years after the death of Tyndale, Henry VIII decreed that Miles Coverdale's English Bible, based largely on Tyndale's translation, must be used in every parish church in the country. Vindicated maybe, but the damage was done, his fortunes did not improve. In 1558, on the death of his brother John, he succeeded to the Manor of North Ockendon but could not afford to live there. He died in 1562 and is buried in St Dunstans in the West, in Fleet Street, London. North Ockendon's Church of St Mary Magdelene lies next to the site of the old Manor House. In its Poyntz Chapel, dedicated in the will of John Poyntz to 'Our Lady', the family are remembered. Thomas' son, Sir Gabriel Poyntz, twice Lord Lieutenant of Essex under Elizabeth I, restored the family fortunes. He commissioned the tomb effigies of himself and his wife and also a series of wall tablets commemorating his

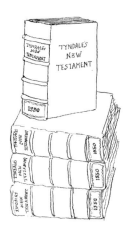

ancestors, including Thomas, which survive today. The church also boasts 'The Poyntz Singers' who are the present day church choir.

In 1604 King James I authorized the First Westminster Company, under the directorship of Lancelot Andrewes, to begin a new translation of the Bible into English. It was finished in 1611, just 85 years after Tyndale's translation appeared. The King Jame's Bible quickly became, and remains, the standard for English speaking Protestants. It has also had a profound influence on English literature.

Lancelot Andrewes was born in Barking in 1555 and later lived at Chichester Hall (now the Chichester Hotel) in the village of Rawreth. At the age of 16 Andrewes entered Pembroke Hall, Cambridge. After graduation his reputation as a scholar grew rapidly. He took orders and served as a chaplain of Queen Elizabeth I and was appointed Dean of Westminster. He served at the coronation of James I and was consecrated as Bishop of Chichester.

In 1605 the 'Gunpowder Plot', to blow up the Houses of Parliament and assassinate King James, was foiled. Andrewes, asked to prepare a sermon for the king, delivered it and called for a lasting celebration of the king's deliverance. This sermon was the inspiration for, and foundation of, the celebrations of Guy Fawkes Day on November 5th which still continue today.

The DISSOLUTION and RICHARD RICHE

In his split from the Papacy, after the Act of Supremacy in 1534, King Henry VIII decreed that all monasteries in England would be closed and their assets confiscated or otherwise disposed of. This action would confirm Henry as head of the Church in England, break the power of the Church of Rome once and for all and also, importantly for the king, replenish his depleted war chest. As a result the crown acquired all monastic lands amounting to approximately one third of the country. Supervised by Thomas Cromwell, Richard Riche was made Chancellor of the Court of Augmentations. His career was meteoric by the standards of the day. Before the age of 40, he would become MP for Colchester then Solicitor General and would eventually rise from a plain Master Riche, to Sir, then Lord and finally Baron Riche of Leez.

In his position as Chancellor of the Court of Augmentations, a post created to raise money from the sale of lands and estates the crown didn't want, Richard Riche, in masterminding these transactions became extremely wealthy. Many of the properties that passed through the Chancellor's office 'stuck to his hands'. Riche lived up to his name in acquiring at least a hundred manors in Essex alone. Apart from Leez Priory and Felsted, they included Fyfield, most of Rochford (that included Hadleigh Castle) and large areas of present day Thurrock. Leez Priory, close to Felsted in Essex, one of the estates to be sold by the crown, was acquired by Riche under somewhat dubious circumstances. The usual procedure was that a King's Agent would visit the monastery in question to value it and report back to the officials at the court. However sometimes gangs of 'persuaders' might be sent along to ensure that a desired valuation was arrived at. They would also arrange acquisition to take place according to a timetable set by the successful purchaser, in this case Chancellor Riche. Leez Priory was originally an Augustinian monastery occupying land by the river Ter, built by Sir Ralph Gernon shortly after the Magna Carta was signed. Riche later constructed an enormous mansion on the site and made the priory his baronial seat.

Riche held high office throughout the reigns of Henry VIII, Edward VI, Queen Mary and well into Elizabeth's time. The young Queen Elizabeth I was a guest in his home at Leez.

Throughout his career Richard Riche was adept at changing sides; he had the knack of knowing when to keep a low profile and skilfully managed to always stay on the right side of the king or queen through four reigns. He was complicit in garnering evidence against many opponents of the reigning monarch, his testimony more than once resulting in executions. In the last year of Henry's reign he is even alleged to have personally tortured the religious reformer, Anne Askew, on the rack before she was burnt at the stake. Baron Riche was made Lord Chancellor during the reign of the young King Edward.

He resigned a year before Edward's death only to come out of retirement a year later to involve himself in the succession of Mary, daughter of Henry VIII and Catherine of Aragon. The devoutly catholic Mary, in trying to undo Henry and Edward's protestant reforms, zealously pursued her religious convictions. Over 250 heretics were burnt at the stake during her rule. All the time Richard Riche was by her side.

When Queen Elizabeth succeeded Mary, Baron Riche changed his allegiance yet again. Approaching his 70th year, he had mellowed and begun his charitable work, perhaps in atonement for previous sins. This included founding the school and alms houses in the village of Felsted, which stand there today. He died in his own bed in his home at Rochford on June 12th 1567. His surviving son and heir, Robert, was with him, as were his daughters Joan, Agnes, Dorothy and Francis. Riche was one of the great survivors. In those turbulent times reaching seventy was quite an achievement. Many of his peers found their way to the block, or were burned at the stake, much earlier.

Baron Riche lay in state for almost four weeks whilst funeral preparations were made. Hundreds of people came to pay their respects, many staying on in Rochford to accompany the funeral procession. The coffin was transported on a chariot draped in black and decorated with the Riche coat of arms and heraldic symbols. The hearse was followed by a mounted escort consisting of one hundred knights and gentlemen and three hundred yeomen all dressed in black. It proceeded slowly, passing by some of Riche's Essex properties in Hawkwell, Rayleigh and Chelmsford to arrive at Felsted Parish Church, where he was laid to rest alongside his wife Elizabeth, who had died nine year earlier. Like much else in Riche's life there is nothing modest in his funeral chapel in the church. His monument is over 12 feet high. Immediately in front of his imposing figure stands a smaller statute of his son Robert, the second Baron Riche.

PIE POWDER COURT SITTING

The charge, false weight and measures my lord
We have a witness here who will testify to fraud.

In spite of all the intrigue and plotting surrounding Queen Elizabeth I and threats to the nation from abroad, most of the population tried, as far as possible, to carry on with their lives and businesses as normal. For some people normal business was sharp practice, fraud and deception. For others their job was to apprehend cheats, prosecute them and in general to see justice done.

In 1566 Richard Asser found himself before what was known as the 'Pie Powder' Court in the Moot Hall in Maldon. The term 'Pie Powder' is assumed to have been derived from the 'Old' French *pieds poudreux*, a term that referred to the dusty feet of travelling traders. The courts had unlimited jurisdiction for all events taking place in the market, including disputes between traders, theft and acts of violence. According to William Blackstone in his *Commentaries on the Laws of England*, published in the 1760s, "They existed because of the necessity for speedy justice over people who were not permanent residents of the place where the market was held".

Richard Asser was one such travelling salesman who traded in a number of Essex markets. He was before the court after being discovered using false weights and measures. Court records of the day also showed that three shoemakers and two saddlers appeared, charged with displaying goods of poor quality.

As a punishment the sale items were seized, valued and sold. The money realised was divided into thirds and shared between the market inspectors, the court and the poor. The false weights and measures likewise would have been confiscated. The rogue trader, Richard Asser, would probably have suffered an additional fine and possibly a spell in the stocks. Pie Powder courts first started 200 years before Mr Asser's time. The authority to convene the courts was written into the Royal charters, which enabled the local Lord of the Manor to hold markets on his lands.

The last known sitting of a Pie Powder Court was in Bristol in 1870, although the rights to hold them were not taken off the statute book until 1977. Today national trading standards are enshrined in law. Market disputes fall within the jurisdiction of the local authority and are overseen by Market Inspectors, backed up by the Police and local Magistrates courts as necessary.

HARBINGERS AT HARLOW

The trumpeters sounded and pealing church bells
Announced the arrival of Good Bess, their Queen.
Outriders in scarlet and gold spangled livery
Heralded such sights before never seen.

In an age without mass communication Queen Elizabeth I cultivated the goodwill of her subjects by means of annual 'progressions'. These tours of different parts of the country were principally designed to allow her to see, and be seen by, her people. They generally took place during the summer months and involved the whole court, as many as five hundred people on the move for weeks at a time.

On three of these progressions through Essex, in September 1571, August 1576 and July 1578, Elizabeth stayed at Mark Hall in Latton, the home of James Altham, Sheriff of Essex, and his wife Lady Mary Judd. It was an honour to be chosen, albeit an expensive one, as their standing in the community would be enhanced considerably.

Weeks before the intended visit royal inspectors called 'harbingers' would be sent to the hosts to ensure that their accommodation was fit for the queen. Meeting their standards could mean a lot of work and expense, from rearranging furniture to redecorating or even re-building if things were not to their liking. The 'harbingers' arrival brought panic followed by frenzied activity and the queen's stay could mean financial hardship or even ruin if the visit went badly. Hence the modern day phrase, 'harbingers of doom'.

As the progression approached Mark Hall people from the villages of Latton, Harlow, Nettleswell and Parndon would have gathered to see their queen. It would have been a grand and colourful sight; heralds followed by trumpeters, their fanfares competing with cheering and the peal of bells from St Mary-at-Latton. The court would levy fines if the bells were not rung for the queen. Finally Elizabeth would ride up in her finery to be greeted by her hosts and local dignitaries. Speeches would be made and gifts exchanged, in all there would be something of a carnival atmosphere.

Mark Hall is remembered in Harlow today by two districts bearing the name, Mark Hall North and Mark Hall South. Most of the Hall was burned down in 1947. The surviving wing, which became a primary school, was demolished in 1960.

JUST MAD ABOUT SAFFRON

As far as the eye could see saffron grew,
Shining purple and white in the morning dew.

It is generally accepted that the word saffron is derived from the Arabic Za'faran. Saffron is taken from the stigma of the saffron crocus, Crocus Sativus. In normal conditions it flowers between September and November. Saffron was a highly prized commodity used for flavouring, dyeing and medicinal purposes and buyers would travel great distances to acquire it.

The plant was introduced into Essex during Norman times. Walden was an ideal place to grow such a crop as the soil was good and the climate favourable. Although not much saffron was actually grown in the confines of Walden, the town became the centre of the commerce associated with it. Wool was a major product in England and the demand for saffron dye was enormous. There was also a flourishing spice trade. Soon Walden became known as Chipping (meaning market) Walden. In the plant's honour, the town's name was changed to Saffron Walden. The earliest documented evidence of this is 1582.

There may also have been a regal connection with the name change. Sir Thomas Smith, a Walden man by birth, was Secretary of State to Queen Elizabeth I. As with all industries there are periodic ups and downs. Sir Thomas Smith sought to revive the fortunes of the town, perhaps by suggesting a name change as a marketing ploy. It could be said in modern parlance that it was an early form of corporate re-branding!

The workers who harvested the crop were known as Crokers. Each flower had three stigmas which had to be plucked by hand. 75,000

flowers were needed to produce one pound of spice. The market for local saffron gradually declined, with cheaper foreign alternatives available and a growing reluctance to use it for medicinal purposes. The final nail in its coffin was the collapse of the English woollen industry in the 1700s. However the name Saffron Walden lives on - with no plans to change it in the near future as far as we know.

A WEAK AND FEEBLE WOMAN

'I know I have the body of a weak and feeble woman,'
the nobles looked on as the Queen began,
And all those kneeling rose as one to stand,
'But I have the heart and stomach of a king of England.'

The words, 'I know I have the body of a weak and feeble woman,' were spoken by Queen Elizabeth I on a windswept field in West Tilbury on the 9th August 1588. These were perhaps the most inspirational words ever recorded by a monarch of England when the kingdom was under threat.

A day earlier the queen had arrived at Tilbury Fort, travelling by royal barge from London. With her entourage she made her way to Saffron Gardens, just south of Horndon-on-the-Hill, where she spent the night. The following day Elizabeth headed for the great military camp set up adjacent to the present day Gunn Hill farm. Befitting the occasion the queen rode up, marshal's baton in her hand, clad in white armour on a grey charger. The Earls of Essex and Leicester held the bridle-rein. Assembled were more than 20,000 soldiers standing by to repel any land invasion unleashed from Armada ships.

The queen spoke with an unmatched passion. 'Let tyrants fear - I come amongst you, not for recreation or sport' and famously offered 'in the midst and heat of the battle, to live or die amongst you all.' Angrily the queen poured scorn on the papal forces that would dare invade England. To strengthen defences a boom had been constructed across the Thames between Gravesend and Tilbury to prevent enemy vessels making up-stream to London. The watch ships *Victory* and *Lyon* patrolled at strategic points further down the estuary to intercept suspicious craft and the church towers at Fobbing and Leigh-on-Sea served as look out points with their beacon turrets ready to be fired if invaders were spotted.

Ironically the great speech made by Queen Elizabeth took place when much of the threat from the Spanish had been neutralised. Originally the Armada set sail from Lisbon, with 130 ships and some 30,000 men, in early July. However the English, through a combination of superior intelligence, better ships and seamanship, together with favourable weather and good luck saw the defeat of the Armada by July 29th. As the prospect of invasion receded most of the troops at Tilbury were withdrawn in late August. The remnants of the Armada finally limped home in mid-September, battered by gales, having lost half the fleet and most of its men.

THE FATHER OF ENGLISH MUSIC
IN STONDON MASSEY

'William Byrd was a musical phenomenon
Throughout Europe acknowledged supreme.
Without him musicians, from Elgar to Elton,
Would not have known where to begin.'

William Byrd's lifetime spanned the reign of five monarchs, Henry VIII, Edward VI, Mary, Elizabeth I and James I. This was a period of considerable turmoil especially if, like Byrd, one was a Roman Catholic. He is acknowledged as one of the great masters of the late renaissance and by some as the greatest English composer ever.

Brought to the attention of Queen Elizabeth, he accepted a position in the Royal Chapel. A known Catholic in a vehemently Protestant England, he was always discrete. His loyalty to the crown was never in question and he enjoyed the favour of the queen. Elizabeth awarded him, jointly with Thomas Tallis his onetime teacher, the monopoly on music publishing. That he was allowed to keep this, even after the death of Tallis, is a measure of his status.

He wrote a great deal of sacred songs in Latin which was banned. They could only be performed in secret Catholic services held in private residences. These were frequently held in Ingatestone Hall, the seat of the Petre family. Sir John Petre, Byrd's wealthiest patron, Sheriff of Essex and First Lord of Writtle, was also a Roman Catholic. Religion of choice, it would seem, could be followed as long as it wasn't obvious.

After retiring from the Royal Chapel at the age of fifty, Byrd went to live in Stondon Massey, a small village close to Ingatestone. A further factor in his choice of Stondon Massey may have been that it was one of three parishes in that part of Essex where Roman Catholicism was fairly strong. Services were held, albeit behind closed doors, in many private houses throughout the Elizabethan years of persecution.

Byrd acquired Stondon Place in 1593 where he lived until his death thirty years later. It has been said that during this period he composed some of his finest music. The previous owner of Stondon Place was William Shelley who had been implicated in a plot to overthrow the queen. He was sentenced to death but later reprieved. The original Stondon Place, a large farmhouse, was rebuilt in 1770 and again after a fire in 1880.

Castle Hedingham seat of the de Vere Family

ESSEX BOY and GIRLS?

There can be little doubt that William Shakespeare came from Stratford-upon-Avon. Born to John and Mary Shakespeare he was baptised on the 26th April 1564, three days after his birth, now accepted as 23rd April. He may have attended Stratford Grammar school; though no records survive he would seem to have been educated somewhere. He married Anne Hathaway in 1582. Or should it have been Anna Whately? There

are entries in the episcopal register at Worcester for licences granted for both. Was it a clerical error or a late change to a shotgun wedding, as it is known that Hathaway was pregnant when they married? What happened later now supports a huge industry of theatre, tourism and Shakespeare memorabilia in Stratford and the wider world.

William Shakespeare is credited with having written 154 sonnets, 34 plays and 2 epic poems. To suggest that the true author of these is in fact someone else from Essex would seem preposterous. Many of his contemporaries, actors, fellow writers, such as Ben Johnson and Christopher Marlow and theatre owners like John Heminge and Henry Condell, freely acknowledged Shakespeare's talents. And yet, for nearly three centuries various groups of people have argued that Shakespeare was not the true author of these works. The candidates variously proposed as the real author have included the philosopher Sir Francis Bacon, the playwright Christopher Marlow, William Stanley Earl of Derby, Roger Manners Earl of Rutland and Sir Henry Neville.

Today the most persistent candidate to be the 'true bard', the subject Thomas J Looney's 1920 book, 'Shakespeare Identified', and championed by 'The Shakespeare Oxford Society', among others, has been Edward de Vere, the 17th Earl of Oxford, whose family seat was Hedingham Castle, Essex. Unlikely though this claim may seem, it is known that de Vere supporters point to Shakespeare's humble beginnings and lack of evidence documenting the education he must have had. He never left England and travel within the country seems to have been limited. So, they ask, how did he know the details of court procedures and intrigues for the historical plays? Where did his knowledge of Italy, Denmark and Scotland, crucial to some of his plots, come from? Edward de Vere, on the other hand, was an accomplished poet, well educated, spoke several languages and had travelled all over England and Europe, particularly Italy. His brother-in-law was well acquainted with Denmark, giving him an insight into the Danish court, necessary for the plot of Hamlet. As a boy he was a royal ward of Richard Cecil (Lord Burley), chief advisor to Queen Elizabeth I., he had consorted with foreign ambassadors and the like and was well known at court. He had also entertained Queen Elizabeth at Castle Hedingham.

Very few hard facts of Shakespeare's life were recorded. Sometime after 1590, the actor William Shakespeare performed with the Lord Chamberlain's Men and other theatre troupes in London, possibly in front of Queen Elizabeth I. In 1597 William Shakspeare (there are many different spellings of his name) bought a large house in Stratford-on-Avon, where, in 1616, he died aged 52. He left no manuscripts, drafts or even letters and the only samples of his handwriting are six different signatures, including the one on his will. Much of the rest of his life is guesswork and speculation and, apart from London to Stratford-on-Avon, he travelled very little. So if not Shakespeare what evidence is there for de Vere as the true author of the literary legacy we enjoy today?

Edward de Vere was a noted court poet as well as a writer of plays. A few of his poems survive but sadly none of his plays do. While there are some parallels in his life with storylines in Shakespeare's plays, particularly Romeo and Juliet, if he drew on these to write the plays why publish them under the pseudonym of William Shakespeare? One answer may be that in Elizabethan time, reinterpreting history in performance was highly dangerous if it was thought to reflect adversely on the queen or her favourites. Elizabeth I had recognized the power of the theatre for propaganda purposes. In 1586 she awarded de Vere an annuity of £1,000; a huge sum of money. Was this to allow de Vere to withdraw from court life and spend his time writing, producing the works that bear the name William Shakespeare?

The most compelling evidence against the Oxfordian Theory is that de Vere died in 1604, whereas approximately twelve of Shakespeare's plays are generally accepted to have been written after that date; the first folio was not published until 1623.

No doubt the arguments will continue to rumble on. Popular interest in the Oxfordian theory persists, and in the eyes of many people the idea that Hedingham Castle in Essex is the true home of Shakespeare's plays, though not provable, is at least as plausible as any of the many other theories. Edward de Vere's candidacy for the title of the 'True Bard' was given a boost when he was played by Rhys Ifans in the 2011 film Anonymous (directed by Roland Emmerich), which explored the subject Hollywood style!

Earlier in the book we mentioned Robert de Vere who was one of the rebel Magna Carta barons. He died on 25th October 1221 and was buried at Hatfield Priory. For 500 years successive de Veres played prominent roles in English history. In 1703 Aubrey, the 20th Earl of Oxford, died childless and the title was no more. The estates were broken up and one part was inherited by a linen draper in London, Edward Rigby, whose family had a profound effect on the village of Mistley, on the river Stour. (see page 82)

It would seem opportune to now mention Maid Marion (of Robin Hood fame). The legend of Robin Hood was born during the chaos and banditry of the time of King John and the Magna Carta. There is a story that Maid Marion was the daughter of the leader of the Magna Carta barons, Robert Fitzwalter (the Lord of Dunmow). Matthew Paris the 13th century chronicler wrote in his diary; 'FitzWalter had a daughter, Matilda the Fair, called 'Maid Marion,' said to have been poisoned by King John'.

The legend has it that Matilda (Marion) married Robin, Earl of Huntingdon (Robin Hood) after rejecting the advances of King John. John, not one to accept rejection, allegedly poisoned Matilda (Marion) by sending her a poisoned bracelet which killed her. Marion, or Matilda, is buried in the Priory Church in Little Dunmow in Essex.

CANVEY DUTCH COTTAGE

Wooden clogs wait on the fender
As though their owner still lived here.
A tribute to Vermmuyden's skilful past
Designed by this Dutchman – built to last.

The Canvey Dutch Cottage Museum on Canvey Road serves as a monument to Dutch influences on the island's early development. Probably built in 1618 by Dutchman Julius Sludder, it was a teashop during the 1950s. Previously it had been home to a family of eight. It is one of two surviving cottages. The other, dated 1621, is still a private house.

Their design was unique for the time. Most English dwellings of that size would almost certainly have been built of wood, whereas these cottages were built with brick, small industrial type bricks unknown in England at that time and probably imported from Holland. Their octagonal shape was unusual. In one of the cottages a number of cartwheels were discovered embedded in the earth floor, arranged around, and all touching a central wheel. This formation has been found in the Netherlands in the base of some types of wind and water mills as well as in some Flemish horse mills.

The cottages were built just before the first serious attempt at land reclamation and protection from the encroaching sea. In the early seventeenth century the principal landowners on the island were Sir Henry Appleton and Abigail Baker. However secondary but sizeable lands were also owned by John, William and Mary Blackmore, Thomas Bincker and Julius Sludder mentioned above. In 1623 Sir Henry Appleton proposed a project to reclaim land from the sea, which would protect their existing land and expand their holdings. The project would be financed by Appleton's associate, Joas Croppenburg, a wealthy London merchant. In return Croppenburg would take ownership of one third of all the reclaimed land. This share was to become known as the 'Third Acre Lands'.

Joas Croppenburg was related to Cornelius Vermuyden, a young Dutch engineer who was acquiring a growing reputation. Vermuyden was in England to oversee the restoration of a breach in the sea wall at Dagenham. He had also been responsible for projects of drainage and land reclamation in the East Anglian Fens.

Engaged to organise the Canvey project, Vermuyden brought three hundred workmen from Holland to build the new sea walls and drain the reclaimed land. His skill and the success of the project were recognised when, knighted by King Charles I, he became Sir Cornelius Vermuyden.

He is remembered and commemorated to this day by the Canvey School that bears his name.

Many of the Dutch workers were paid with grants of 'Third Acre' land and settled on Canvey Island with their families. They had much work to do before they could reap the benefits of farming their land. The cost of maintaining the sea walls, though high, was one they bore willingly to protect their investment in their new lives. Some of the English so-called 'Freeland' owners however were not quite so meticulous in keeping to their obligations which resulted in flooding which disheartened their neighbours. Over time some Dutchmen sold up and moved away. Those that stayed formed the nucleus of a strong, and lasting, Dutch influence on the island.

By the late eighteenth century the sea walls had again deteriorated. A season of fierce tides breached the walls causing severe damage in 1791. The following year Parliament was petitioned with an act for "effectively embanking, draining and otherwise improving the Island of Canvey in the County of Essex". Since then the sea defences have been more or less continually upgraded and especially so since they were overwhelmed in the floods of 1953 (see page 184, the Great Surge). Areas of Canvey Island have since suffered flooding but on every occasion since 1953 this has been due to heavy rainfall and the inability of the pumps to remove excess water quickly enough.

In the early 20th century Canvey Island had about 500 residents. The numbers grew steadily after the first road bridge was opened in 1931.

BILLERICAY PIONEERS

They abandoned their roots for a New World life,
Fleeing persecution and intolerance which under
King James' rule was rife.

The Mayflower, under its master Christopher Jones of Harwich,  set sail from Plymouth on the 6ᵗʰ September 1620. It was headed for the 'New World' across the Atlantic Ocean. With a crew of 35, the Mayflower carried 102 pioneers, now known as the 'Pilgrim Fathers'. One of them died on the voyage and one new 'Pilgrim' was born. Landfall at Cape Cod, in present day Massachusetts, was achieved 66 days later after an arduous 2,750 nautical mile journey. Amongst the group were four from Billericay, Essex: Christopher Martin, his wife Marie, step-son Solomon Prower and their servant John Langmore. They became known as the Billericay Pioneers. It is quite possible that the four joined the *Mayflower* at Leigh-on-Sea.

Christopher Martin was an enigma. He ran a victualling, or wholesale food, business and may have been a miller. There is evidence that he owned properties in the Billericay area. By all accounts he was a difficult man to deal with, often clashing with traders, local authorities, the church and even fellow worshippers. Perhaps he thought joining the 'Pilgrims' could be a business opportunity or did he just want to get away from people he didn't get on with? Whatever his reasons Martin somehow became treasurer for the 'Mayflower Pilgrims' and became responsible for organising provisions for the voyage. Surprisingly, he was also elected to be governor of the first colony.

Before long Martin fell out with almost everyone. His haughty attitude and refusal to supply accounts plus his uncoordinated way of acquiring stores was a constant irritant to the pilgrims and their sponsors. Just before the *Mayflower* was due to sail things came to a head. His fellow 'Pilgrims' overwhelmingly passed a vote of no confidence and replaced him as governor. In spite of this Christopher Martin still chose to go.

Within three months of making landfall, half of the Pilgrims, including all those from Billericay, died in the harsh winter conditions. Nevertheless the new colony survived. In the following years further ships arrived bringing more pilgrims from Essex to begin a new life. Thus the colony prospered and one of the foundations of the new American nation was laid.

The pilgrims differed from other colonists. They were not going to the New World to seek their fortune but to escape religious persecution

and be able to live according to their strict puritan Christian beliefs. Their voyage was financed by enterprising groups of Merchant Adventurers who saw the 'Pilgrims' as advance parties or 'shock troops' in developing colonies that in the long term would give scope for future profit.

The 'Pilgrims' were not the first group from England to cross the Atlantic. In 1585 Sir Walter Raleigh brought 100 settlers to Roanoke Island in Chesapeake Bay, in present day Virginia. Two years later all trace of them had gone. Roanoke had become the lost colony. In 1607 another settlement was founded in the same area. It was another

Harwich man, Christopher Newport who captained the small flotilla that took these colonists to what today is Jamestown. Despite the relatively benign environment this colony only just survived.

The legacy of these Essex pilgrims still persists in Massachusetts today. Within the state there is not only an Essex County and the town of Essex, there is also a Chelmsford, a Braintree, a Harwich and a Billerica - although it mysteriously lost its 'y' whilst crossing the Atlantic.

Captain Jones's house still stands in Harwich. Inside the *Mayflower Tavern and Restaurant* in the 'old town' of Leigh-on-Sea there is wooden plaque recording all the names of those who sailed on the original *Mayflower*.

SAY 'I DO, PAY THE FEE, SIGN THE BOOK'

The false name she gave was the one he took;
'Just pay the fee, say 'I do' and sign the book.''

It is often said that trouble comes in threes. Gilbert Dillingham, Brian Walton and Samuel Smith succeeded each other as Rectors of St Andrews Church, Sandon near Chelmsford, and proved the rule rather than the exception.

Just over 400 years ago, in 1601, Gilbert Dillingham took up his position and moved into the rectory. The reign of Queen Elizabeth was drawing to a close and the new monarch would be James I. For the first time in the history of the British Isles the crowns of England and Scotland would be united.

For Dillingham, like all past rectors at Sandon, the office held many benefits. Comfortable lodgings were provided together with a reasonable income from the tithe. This was a 10% tax levied on the profits from land and stock falling within the parish. Gifts from wealthy benefactors were also added to the church coffers as well as the plate collections and fees from weddings, christening and funeral services. Furthermore, in the early 1600s church attendance was compulsory for all parishioners.

On the surface Gilbert Dillingham appeared quite content with his lot and for 14 years nothing much changed. However the Rector was working on a scheme to boost his income from weddings. Prior to 1615, St Andrews Church hosted an average of four weddings a year. Word spread quickly of the rector's new scheme and suddenly, almost overnight, Sandon was the place to go to be married quickly. With 'Instant Weddings' on offer, lovesick grooms and would be brides were heading for Sandon from far and wide. Few questions were asked and little if anything was done to verify the answers given. In many cases false names were used and many 'Mr and Mrs Smiths' departed happily after the ceremony. Gilbert Dillingham's biggest coup was to marry off the daughter of a neighbouring vicar. There was only one condition - the wedding fee was to be promptly paid on the day.

During his tenure the Reverent Dillingham conducted over 500 weddings. So while Gretna Green* or even Las Vegas spring to mind as places for couples looking for a quick way to tie the knot it was Sandon in

Essex that pioneered the quickie wedding. In 1636 Gilbert Dillingham retired and was never heard of again.

Brian Walton, the next rector, was a biblical scholar. He took his duties very seriously and was baffled when couples who had no connection with the parish began turning up hoping for a speedy wedding. Walton, who wanted to move on to greater things in the church hierarchy, immediately put a stop to the wedding business much to the consternation of his would be customers. The new rector did not hold his post for long though. In 1641 the dark clouds of the English Civil war were looming and Walton, as a committed royalist was 'removed'. He fled to staunchly royalist Oxford shortly afterwards.

The next rector appointed at Sandon was Samuel Smith. Contemporary records describe him as a very low churchman. He had a puritanical outlook much in tune with the ascendant Cromwellian values of the day. Smith was rector for nearly 20 years. In that time he managed to upset many of the congregation and was enthusiastic in summoning them for non-attendance. Although the previous rector, Brian Walton, was supposedly on the run, he still tried to get his hands on the tithe income from Sandon. It is difficult to imagine, bearing in mind the primitive communications of the time, how he could achieve his objective. Walton's efforts sufficiently annoyed Samuel Smith to prompt him to write a letter of complaint to a Parliamentary committee. The committee, being no friend of royalist sympathisers, immediately issued a warrant for Walton's arrest.

More drama was to follow at the Sandon Rectory. In 1660, following the death of Oliver Cromwell, the monarchy was restored. Now Samuel Smith was out of favour. Orders were given to 'remove' him. However Smith decided he would have none of it and barricaded himself in. All attempts at persuasion to leave were rejected and eventually the bailiffs were called. They broke in through the rectory roof and dragged him out.

Theoretically Brian Walton was restored as rector but a greater calling came. He took up the post of chaplain to King Charles II and was then elevated to Bishop of Chester. As for Sandon rectory, the last of the troublesome occupants had gone. William Wells became rector and church affairs have remained calm ever since.

Gretna Green did not become a 'Wedding destination' until 1754.

LEIGH FISHY TALES.

Legends abound of smuggled brandy and tea
And Leigh men have always lived from the sea
Some became Admirals and were highly revered
While some were 'pressed' many more volunteered.

The raised brick tomb of Mary Ellis with its flat altar stone topping, standing just outside the entrance porch of St Clement's Church, bears the epitaph, *Here lies the body of Mary Ellis, daughter of Thomas & Lydia Ellis of this parish. She was a virgin of virtuous courage & promising hope and died on the 3rd of June 1609, aged 119.*

Amusing as this is, the strange markings on top of the altar stone tell a less amusing story. The seventeenth century was the beginning of the age of the dreaded naval press gangs. The Navy was desperately short of men and places like Leigh-on-Sea, with a strong fishing tradition, were prime recruiting grounds. When unable to meet their quotas elsewhere the press gangs, on Sundays, would sometimes wait in St Clement's churchyard for men to emerge from the service. They would stand around Mary Ellis's tomb and while waiting sharpen their cutlasses on its top, thus giving it its nickname of 'The Cutlass Stone'. Fortunately for the young men of Leigh the noise of sharpening could be heard in the church warning them of impending danger. They quickly then disappeared down a hidden underground tunnel to the cellar of the rectory where they would await the all clear from the sexton. The press gangs would watch disappointedly as the congregation emerged, consisting only of women, children and old men well passed naval service.

How much of this story is true and how much legend is a matter of conjecture. What cannot be inferred from it is that the men of Leigh were averse to serving their country. History is littered with the names of Leigh men who rose to fame by doing their duty. The Haddock family, residents of Leigh for four hundred years, came to fame in the seventeenth century when William Haddock became Commander of *The America* fighting against the Dutch in 1653.

Perhaps the most famous Haddock was Richard, also a captain in the Navy. He commanded *The Royal James* and was wounded at the battle of Sole Bay in 1672. Subsequently promoted to Admiral and Comptroller of the Navy, he also represented Aldeburgh in parliament in 1678. He became MP for Shoreham in 1685-7, as well as being Master of Trinity House. His eldest son, another Richard, was also to become Comptroller of the Navy. Nicholas, his younger son, was created Admiral of the Blue in 1744.

The Salmon family lived in Leigh for three hundred years and between 1588 and 1641 three generations, all named Robert, were Masters of Trinity House.

Another Leigh family, the Goodlads, were shipbuilders to Queen Elizabeth the first. William Goodlad, who commanded the Greenland Fleet for twenty years, was also Master of Trinity House when he died in 1638. There seems to have been something of a tradition of Leigh men becoming Masters of Trinity House. Richard Chester, who lived on Strand Wharf, was appointed to the role in 1615.

Much later William Brand from Leigh commanded *The Revenge* and fought with Nelson at Trafalgar. For centuries Leigh men have played a part in our seafaring traditions, right up to modern times when the *Little Ships of Leigh* sailed to Dunkirk. (see page 174)

Of course there are other aspects to the endeavours of Leigh's men of the sea. Ever since excise duties were introduced smuggling has been practised. Leigh, with its shallow tidal creeks and marshes, was a smugglers' haven. The Custom House in Leigh was built on Strand Wharf in 1738, although the first customs officer was appointed in 1565. Since then, and into the nineteenth century, Leigh fishermen have played hide and seek with the excise men. Some of today's well-known families claim ancestors that made a good living from smuggling. One of the more successful smugglers was George Walter, whose father Edward Newton Walter was rector of St Clement's Church. George, a retired Marine Officer, organised the local sailors so that their operations were like military manoeuvres. His father, the rector, and other dignitaries were always looked after with a token share of the contraband. Rumours persist to this day of secret tunnels built to evade the customs. One of these was proven when in 1892 fire broke out in 'The Peterboat' tavern. It was burnt to the ground, exposing a secret cellar beneath the main cellar, with direct access to the waterfront, where contraband goods were stored then moved through secret trapdoors house to house in Old Leigh.

Smuggling rewards were high but the penalties, if caught, were equally severe. At times the smugglers were offered an amnesty in return for volunteering to serve three years in the Navy. Unsurprisingly there is little evidence of this happening on any scale in Leigh.

WITCH-FINDER GENERAL

With elegant long necks and stately progress
The swans in numbers glide, from Manningtree to Mistley
Along the river Stour both clear and wide.

For centuries swans have been gliding gracefully on the River Stour between Mistley and Manningtree witnessing all around. Back in the seventeenth century this north east corner of Essex was a hotbed of Puritan support for Oliver Cromwell's Roundheads in the raging English Civil War. Against this turmoil Matthew Hopkins set himself up as Witch-Finder General and in 1645 he began a campaign of terror, mostly against poor and vulnerable women. Much of what is known of Hopkins is speculative. No known records exist of his birth, early years and education. He was probably born in Mistley around 1619. The only record of his death is a note in a book published in 1854 quoting an ancient parish register from 1559; *Matthew Hopkins, son of Mr James Hopkins, Minister of Wenham, was buried at Mistley, August 12th, 1647.*

Hopkins was assisted in his fourteen-month reign of terror by 'Witch-Pricker'* John Sterne. Together they were responsible for the condemnation and execution of more than 200 alleged witches. Hopkins first 'case' was to accuse Elizabeth Clarke, a poor one-legged woman whose mother had been hanged as a witch. He personally interrogated her with Sterne's help and used torture to obtain a confession that also incriminated five other women. The investigation spread to over a hundred people, gaining more confessions. Eventually thirty two women were tried at a special court in Chelmsford in July 1645. Of these twenty-nine were condemned to the gallows. Four according to Hopkins, were *to be hanged (at Mistley) at where their discoverer (Hopkins) lives.* These were troublesome times and thankfully the witch hysteria died down to a great extent after the sixteen-forties.

Local legend has it that Hopkins' ghost haunts Mistley Pond and a figure in seventeenth century clothing is seen on Friday nights at the time of the Witches Sabbats**.

*Witch-pricker, the assistant who would search an alleged witch for marks of the Devil. ** Witches Sabbats: There are 8 sabbats, 4 major, May Eve, Midsummer Day, Lammas (1st August) and Halloween and 4 lesser, Yule (usually Christmas day), Candlemas (approximately 2 February), Spring Equinox and Fall Equinox.*

UNDER SIEGE

Lucas and Lisle had the Royalist command,
Townspeople in fear of the army's demands.

In 1648 the people of Colchester, in common with most of the population, were fed up with years of civil war. The King, Charles I, had given himself up to Cromwell's Parliamentarians. Yet there were significant pockets of royalist supporters with other ideas. One of them was George Goring, the Earl of Norwich, who had 3,000 men under his command. He was joined by Sir George Lisle with another 2,500 men. Together they made their way to Colchester where they decided to make a stand and fight.

The burghers of Colchester, terrified of occupation, barred the gates and posted sixty guards to prevent access. Sir Charles Lucas, a royalist commander who came from Colchester, charged the gates. The guards fled and on the 9th of June the town was occupied. Colchester now had five and a half thousand extra mouths to feed from scarce resources.

The Parliamentary forces, under General Lord Fairfax, arrived on the 12th of June. Inside the gates the Earl of Norwich then announced to the townspeople that he would take them into His Majesty's protection and fight the enemy. The citizens were trapped within the walls in exactly the situation the burghers had feared. For eleven weeks Colchester was under siege. The Parliamentarians encircled the town, digging trenches and earthworks. By July 1st the town was effectively cut off. Persistent efforts by royalist troops to break out were beaten back. Whatever food there was the army requisitioned, as well as forcibly recruiting townsmen and their weapons. By mid-July horses were being slaughtered for food. In August people were reduced to eating cats, dogs, and even rats. With starvation at hand and no prospect of relief, the royalists surrendered on the 27th of August. When the victors entered the town they were shocked at the sorry state of both the town and the inhabitants. Cruelly there was no sympathy for the people; instead they were fined heavily for allowing the king's men into their town in the first place.

Two royalist commanders, Sir Charles Lucas and Sir George Lisle, were tried and summarily executed by firing squad. Their leader, the Earl of Norwich, escaped with his life, being of the aristocracy his fate was left for Parliament to decide. Many of the surviving rank and file soldiers were savagely treated and subsequently deported to the West Indies to work as slave labour.

DEAR DIARY
AUDLEY END

To view Audley End House in its beautiful grounds,
The whole of the place could not be better found.

Samuel Pepys had a varied and busy life. In 1649 he was present at the execution of Charles I. He lived through English Civil War, the rule of Oliver Cromwell and was an enthusiastic witness to the return of Charles II to the throne in 1660. Pepys survived the Great Plague in London in 1665 and, a year later, The Great Fire of London. He was imprisoned in the Tower, and remarkably, since he never lived there, became the Member of Parliament for Harwich. (See following page)

Pepys had a remarkable career as a naval administrator through very turbulent times. Today he is best remembered for the diary he kept from 1660 to 1669. Never intended for publication, the diaries were written in his own cryptic shorthand. They were discovered 25 years after his death and not translated for publication until almost a century later in 1825.

A diary entry for Monday 27th February 1660 records Pepys' visit to Audley End near Saffron Walden with his friend Mr Blaydon. He describes the house and gardens around as *exceedingly worth seeing,* paying particular attention to the *stateliness of the ceilings, chimney-pieces'* *and the portraits.* During the visit he was invited down to the cellars with  the housekeeper whereupon, *we drank most admirable drink and toasted the Kings health.*

Being an accomplished musician and, *there being an excellent echo*, Pepys, then entertained those present on his *flageolette*. Later he visited the local almshouse, *where forty poor people was maintained*, before adjourning to the local Inn where he proceeded to flirt with the *daughter of the house, she being very pretty*.

During the dissolution, Walden Abbey, was granted to Sir Thomas Audley by Henry VIII. It was demolished by his grandson, Thomas Howard, the first Earl of Suffolk who then built Audley End house on the scale of a great royal palace. Howard fell on hard times and in 1626 Charles II bought the house for £5 to use as a home when attending the races at Newmarket.

Over the years Audley End has been modified and changed many times. In the late 1770s Sir John Griffin Griffin* employed the architect Robert Adams and the landscape gardener Lancelot (Capability) Brown to renovate the house and gardens.

During World War II, the Special Operations Executive used the house as a base for training secret agents. After the war the Ministry of Works purchased the House for £30,000. Today the house and grounds are managed by English Heritage and are open to the public. As a tribute to Samuel Pepys, two abridged volumes of the diaries are kept in the library.

Yes his name really was Sir John Griffin Griffin

ELECTED BY 32

Elections were not considered suitable at that stage,
As for public opinion, that was impossible to gauge.

In the general election of 2005, the parliamentary seat of Harwich and Clacton had an electorate of some 80,000. One Member of Parliament was elected to serve the constituency. There were six candidates. Over

three hundred years ago things were a little different. On 5th February 1679 Harwich, with an adult population of around a mere 800, elected two Members of Parliament. The electoral role was precisely 32. There would seem to have been no other candidates.

The two MPs chosen were the diarist

Samuel Pepys who worked for the admiralty, and Sir Anthony Deane, a master shipwright. The 32 electors were the members of Harwich town council who held office for life, unless they were too ill to carry on or they resigned. They could only be removed from office if found guilty of misdemeanor by their colleagues. Harwich was a truly 'rotten' borough.

In the 17th century Harwich harbour was a good source of revenue from customs dues, growing commercially and strategically important in defence terms. Government Departments, namely the Treasury, the Postmaster General and, as the navy grew in size, the War Office vied with each other to ensure council positions were given to their men. Local agents were employed to ensure that this happened, often using threats, bribes and blackmail to get their way. Samuel Pepys and Sir Anthony Deane both worked for the navy, so having them elected to parliament was quite a coup for their masters in the Admiralty.

In 1679 a Catholic plot to assassinate King Charles II was discovered. Although later found to be a hoax fabricated by Titus Oates, it was widely believed. Pepys and Deane were both caught up in the investigations. They spent two months in the Tower of London on trumped up charges. The charges were later dismissed and on release they were still the MPs for Harwich.

In 1714 the first of the Hanoverians, George I*, became king. Harwich became the preferred port for British Royals travelling back and forth to Germany. Politics however had not changed, nor would they throughout the Hanover dynasty. Harwich would remain a 'Rotten Borough' until after the 1832 first great reform act. This established the principal of election to office by popular vote. By 1835 Harwich council was to be elected by the votes of all male ratepayers owning property worth more than £10 a year in rent. Even so, in 1859 there were only 317 names on the Harwich electoral role. Ten years later Harwich's parliamentary representation was reduced to one. Unsurprisingly these moves to wider democracy met with considerable resistance from some existing office holders.

Over the years Harwich has seen many changes to its electoral boundaries. In the 2010 general election it was split from Clacton. Today the town of Harwich is part of the constituency of Harwich and North Essex with an electorate of over 70,000 and is represented by just ONE Member of Parliament.

George I, although 52nd in line to the throne was the nearest protestant contender.

THE BRICK MAKER OF CHADWELL ST MARY

Daniel Defoe was doing well.
His factory made tiles and bricks to sell.

Daniel Defoe - Writer and Tilbury Tile Manufacturer - was pilloried, and then imprisoned, for sedition. Born to James and Alice Foe, though he may have been adopted, in 1660 or 1661, he would later change his name to the grander sounding Defoe. Charles II was on the throne, religious intolerance stalked the land and plots and counterplots were rife. Then came the great plague followed by the great fire; they were turbulent times.

He was regarded as one of the founders of the English novel. *Robinson Crusoe* and *Moll Flanders* are among his best known books. His political and business career, though full of mystery and intrigue, is probably less well known. At the age of 18 he speculatively bought a long lease on a parcel of land in Tilbury.

He was politically active and five years later in 1685 took part in the unsuccessful Monmouth rebellion against James II. When James was replaced by William III, whom Defoe had supported in his writing, he made many friends in the new order.

Politically astute, Defoe's private life was complex and costly. He maintained three houses and was responsible for at least nine children. As well as his legal wife, Mary Tuffey, with whom he had seven children, he also maintained houses for 'private wife' Elizabeth Sammen in London and 'private wife' Mary Norton in Tilbury.

His business life was also chaotic as he was not the entrepreneur he believed himself to be. Many of his enterprises suffered bad luck, or as some would say, mismanagement, and creditors frequently pursued him. His luck ran out though and in October 1692 he was jailed for bankruptcy with debts of £17,000.

Defoe bounced back and having managed to hang on to his land in Tilbury he scraped together the capital to set up a factory specialising in the manufacture of roof tiles. Through his connections he acquired contracts to supply tiles for prestigious projects such as the new Greenwich Hospital.

Initially the factory flourished and Defoe was able to live in grand style in a large house close to Tilbury Fort with a carriage, a pleasure boat and several servants. His writing, however, distracted him from business. The factory was continually beset by problems. It was grossly overstaffed and badly managed. Its products were considered shoddy, and customer's complaints were ignored.

A prolific writer, Defoe's political connections made him well placed to provide 'expert' comment on politics, business, law and order for which the public had a growing appetite. In 1703 however his satirical pamphlet, *The Shortest Way with Dissenters*, caused fury in the establishment, the church and especially with the new monarch Queen Anne. He was arrested, pilloried and then imprisoned, convicted of sedition.

Being in prison was the final straw and, despite the best efforts of his brother-in-law to save it, the brick factory failed. Daniel Defoe was a hopeless business man but as a talented and prolific writer he is credited with publishing over 560 books and pamphlets and being the father of British journalism. Despite this he died in 1731 alone, in debt and pursued by creditors. His son disposed of the factory and land at Tilbury and today all trace of the original factory has been erased.

Daniel Defoe pilloried for bad debts

STAND AND DELIVER

"Stand and Deliver," these words of dread
Dick Turpin is reputed to have said.

Somehow a myth grew up that has led to Dick Turpin being honoured in the names of dozens of pubs and eateries up and down the country. Further plaudits came through film, television, books and comics depicting him as a latter day Robin Hood who took from the rich and gave to the poor. Even more bizarrely he is acknowledged in dozens of journals and websites connected with the meat and sausage trade!

The real Dick Turpin, born in Hempstead, north Essex in 1705, was totally devoid of glamour. Turpin began employment as an apprentice butcher (hence the meat connection above) and then possibly ran a butchers shop in Thaxted. Allegedly, he involved himself with stolen animals which ended his career in the meat business.

Around 1732 Turpin teamed up with Samuel Gregory in what was to become known as the Gregory or Essex Gang. Over a two year period a series of horrific robberies was committed in Essex and London. The gang had no compunction about torturing or beating their victims or violating any women found on the premises whilst the robbery was in progress.

Large rewards were offered for their capture and one by one the outlaws were apprehended. Turpin though managed to remain at large but with a considerable price on his head. He went to ground, surfacing again in 1737 to team up with another villain known as Matthew (or Tom) King. More robberies followed which often resulted in cold blooded murder. However the net was closing and King was tracked down in Whitechapel, East London. Turpin rode to the rescue but all he achieved was to shoot his accomplice in the melee. On his death bed Tom King confessed all.

Escaping again, Turpin fled north assuming the name John Palmer. In York he was arrested on an unrelated matter and put in jail. Letters he penned to relatives, which were censored, identified him as the real Dick Turpin. Tried and convicted on two indictments, he was sentenced to death. On 7th April, 1739, Dick Turpin was hanged as a common criminal at Knavesmire, York aged 34.

Nearly 100 years later a legend was created through the popular 1834 novel *Rookwood* written by Harrison Ainsworth. The horse 'Black Bess' was a fictional creation of the writer and all the rest is just - let us say 'history'.

WALTON TOWER

Through the mist we see you now
A column of unchanging certainty
Walton Tower blesses us in our sights
As we sail hard across the sea.

Walton Tower is 80 feet high and sits on top of the 70 feet Naze cliffs. Built by Trinity House it was a navigational marker for ships approaching the port of Harwich. That was in 1721 and today it is still a comforting sight to east coast sailors coming back to shore. The Naze, from which Walton takes its name, is an area of headland known for its ancient fossils and unique wildlife. In common with much of the east coast however it fights an ongoing, and losing, battle against the sea. The tower currently stands some 50 feet from the cliff edge. It has been calculated that within twenty years it will be demolished, unless action is taken to stem the alarming rate of erosion of the cliffs.

Past events give some idea of the sea's relentless power. The old Parish Church of All Saints, belonging to the Diocesan estate of London's St Paul's Cathedral, was washed away completely in 1796. This victim of coastal erosion is now called 'Prebenda Consumpta per Mare' (The church eaten by the sea). The waves have now advanced several hundred feet beyond the place where the church once stood. Local legend has it that stormy seas caused coffins to float ashore and that people made good use of the timber. There are even tales of sunken church bells being heard.

Originally farmland, the Naze became a private golf course. During the Second World War it was requisitioned by the ministry of defence as a lookout location and in 1967 the local council purchased the area as a public open space. Since then it has been enjoyed by thousands of visitors and residents every year.

In 1998, the Tower, unique of its kind, but in a dilapidated condition, was bought by a local businessman, Edward Chapman, who restored it to its former glory. The Tower is now a museum, art gallery and café and during the summer months is open daily to visitors. The viewing platform offers magnificent views. The Walton Backwaters, seen clearly from there and adored by generations of small boat enthusiasts, once provided Arthur Ransome with the inspiration for his famous children's adventure story *Swallows and Amazons*.

(See also page 82 Rigbys' Follies)

THE FAIRLOP FRIGATE

Daniel Day was accident prone, road travel made him quiver
A keen sailor, he was much more at home on the river.

Two hundred years ago Hainault forest covered much of present day Ilford, Barkingside and Chigwell. It was also the home of the original Fairlop Oak. One of the largest trees ever seen in Britain, it is thought to have been given that name by Queen Anne on a visit in 1704. It grew on a spot occupied by the present day boathouse at Fairlop Water.

This enormous oak tree stood alone in a vast clearing and was the setting for the Fairlop Fair, which began in earnest in 1725. It became an annual event taking place during the first week in July, and ran almost continually until 1900. Its founder was the jovially eccentric Daniel Day.

Daniel Day was a wealthy man who had earned his fortune in marine engineering. He lived on the river Thames at Wapping but owned some cottages near Fairlop. He made it his business to collect the rents there annually, usually on the first Friday in July. He decided to make this day a special occasion for his friends, his employees and his tenants. Bacon and beans were ordered from a local hostelry and a grand 'beanfeast' was held under the great canopy of the Fairlop Oak.

Within a few years others joined in and gradually the gathering turned into a gigantic fair. There would be puppeteers, circus acrobats and exotic animals on hand to provide entertainment. A market sprang up too, selling sweets, toys and nick knacks. To begin with the fair was described "as most respected and well regulated". In 1736 however the first prosecutions were recorded of stallholders for indulging in gaming and illegal liquor sales.

Daniel Day was nervous of travelling by road. He had been involved in a serious accident when his coach overturned. Accordingly he got his workers to put wheels on a masted boat which was decked out with rigging, flags and bunting. He would travel in style by river as far as possible and then by road for the bean feast. On land the boat, nicknamed the *Fairlop Frigate*, was hauled by a team of six horses and preceded by a marching band.

In the 1750's 100,000 people came to the fair from all over London and the unregulated large crowds caused all sorts of problems. In 1765 the local constabulary reported that, "a great number of people meet in a riotous and tumultuous manner, selling ale and spirituous liquors and keeping tippling booths and gaming tables to the great encouragement of vice and immorality".

Daniel Day died in 1767, aged 84, and was buried a coffin fashioned from a branch that had fallen from the Fairlop Oak. He was buried in St. Margaret's Church yard, Barking. He had originally asked to be buried under the Fairlop Oak but his request was declined.

The Fairlop Oak suffered numerous acts of vandalism, particularly from fires lit inside its trunk by careless picnickers. Gradually the tree died and in 1820 it was blown down by a gale. The Fairlop Oak was no more. The fair however continued to grow, vying with the Derby on Epsom Downs as a semiofficial holiday. 1839 saw one of the biggest crowds ever. 200,000 attended the fair. It was one of the biggest carnivals in London and the roads to the area were jammed. However not everyone approved. The Lord's Day Observance society frowned upon the proceedings as did the Religious Tract Society, a Christian book publisher, who counted 108 drinking booths and 72 gaming tables.

The Fairlop Fair continued on various sites for another fifty years but declined gradually and ceased altogether in 1900. Over the years several Fairlop Frigates were built. One built in 1812 was discovered in a Romford back garden in 1951; the hull was rotten, the wheels missing and the rigging and mast all gone. Today at Fullwell Cross, in the London Borough of Redbridge, there is a public house named New Fairlop Oak. Opposite is another oak tree planted in the same year as the frigate was found.

THE QUEENS PLATE

Stock Road was shut, hotels and inns full.
Schools closed as race day exerted its pull.

On the green just outside Galleywood's Library stands the village sign depicting two jockeys racing. The background shows trees and the top of a church steeple further back. White fencing posts mark the edge of a racetrack. Also visible is what seems to be a VIP grandstand. Horse racing ended at Galleywood in 1935. All that may be seen today of these images are St Michael's church and a few remaining white fencing posts along the side of Stock Road.

For 100 years Galleywood was one of the premier racecourses in the land. 1770 brought royal patronage when King George III promised to pay 100 guineas to the winner of a race. His Queen, Charlotte, offered a silver plate – hence the race title becoming, 'The Queen's Plate'. Race meetings at Galleywood were extremely popular and thousands of people travelled for miles to the events. The course was one of the longest in the country. It circled the village church and for the horses it had a killing uphill finish.

When flat racing was replaced by steeple chasing the course developed a notable tag line:-

Galleywood: Steeple chasing round a real steeple.

With race days came all the fun of the fair. Apart from betting, there were entertainers of all shapes and sizes, prize fighting, cock and dog fighting. There was plenty of casual work on the track. In many instances farm labourers just abandoned their daily toil for the more exciting and relatively well paid work on the track, much to the chagrin of the local farmers. The hotels and inns did a roaring trade and were packed solid. The police were kept busy too as the meetings attracted the usual array of pickpockets and con-men. The coming of the races was also eagerly looked forward to by local children. Schools were closed as a safety precaution because of the sheer numbers of people in the area and the amount of unfamiliar traffic.

In 1862 'The Chelmsford Race Company' was formed. It aimed to run the race meetings in a more organised fashion. The company proposed to build a grandstand and associated accommodation with strict rules as to who could be admitted to the stand. Usually race meetings were held over two days and attracted people of every social class. The first day was reserved for the gentry and their ladies. The second day was thrown open to the farmers, their workers and the townsfolk of Chelmsford.

The fortunes of the racecourse fluctuated over the years, but the First World War brought a rapid decline. The company ceased trading in 1922. The last steeple chase was in 1935. After World War II war housing took over much of the site, yet Galleywood common is still an open public space.

Horse racing came back to Essex, on May 28th 2008, with the grand opening of the new Great Leighs racecourse. Boasting an all-weather floodlit track it was the first Essex course to be built for 80 years and reportedly cost £30 million. Unfortunately its success was short lived. Low spectator numbers and mounting debts led to the course being placed into administration less than a year after it opened. The racing licence was revoked and all racing suspended. The Grandstand was later dismantled and removed.

Seven years later, and with new owners, the Great Leighs course, now renamed as Chelmsford City Racecourse, reopened following a major redevelopment and the approval of The British Horse Racing Authority. After test meetings in January before an invited audience, the first public meeting, on February 1st 2015 attracted approximately 1,000 people to enjoy a flutter at the county's newest horse racing venue.

THREE MILLS AT BATTLESBRIDGE

Here, the confluence of centuries –
Three mills- Three histories of quern and staple –
Ground from their meaning by the tides of traffic.

Two hundred years ago Battlesbridge was a self-contained community with a busy harbour that acted as a logistics centre for Wickford, Rayleigh and most of the villages in the surrounding area. Coal, building materials, the new industrial goods made in London and even newspapers would be brought up the River Crouch for distribution. Vessels would then return loaded with flour, animal feed and agricultural produce from the farms nearby, all of which were needed to fuel London's ever expanding growth.

Battlesbridge was a milling town. The first mill constructed was a tide mill, on the south side of the Crouch, upstream from the bridge. Unfortunately the tide was an unreliable source of power and the venture was not deemed a success. In 1815, in the middle of celebrations commemorating the defeat of Napoleon at Waterloo, disaster struck when a careless worker entered the mill floor carrying a lighted candle. The building caught fire and the blaze severely damaged all the machinery.

The mill fell into disuse and the derelict site was acquired by William Meeson from Grays. Meeson owned quarries and several Thames Barges, the new backbone of transport around south eastern England. He immediately realised the mill's location upstream from the bridge was unsuitable as it restricted waterborne access.

A new mill was built on the north bank of the river east of the bridge. This one was steam driven and it was completed in 1896. This is the building we see today called 'The Old Granary'. During the First World War another mill was built on the opposite, south, bank. Milling was obviously good business. William Meeson died in 1926 and the enterprise was taken over by J & G Matthews.

Fire disaster struck again and the mill on the south bank was completely destroyed. At the time of the fire the tide was out so there were no means of extinguishing the flames. Fire was a real hazard with mills and for a time Battlesbridge had its own fire station.

The mill on the south bank was rebuilt in 1933 but times were changing. The days of the Thames Barges were over as being a primary means of transport and Battlesbridge had lost its strategic importance as a distribution centre.

In 1960 the mills were acquired by British Oils and Cake Mills (BOCM) who made animal feeds. Trade continued to decline and both mills were closed within 5 years. During their time the mills had used water, steam, oil and electricity to power them.

In 1967 Battlesbridge Antiques Centre took over the mill on the north bank. The Centre is now spread around five period buildings housing over 80 dealers and is the largest Antique Centre in Essex.

IT'S NOT CRICKET!

One guard was bayoneted and the sergeant shot dead
Before Kent took to their boats and the Essex men fled.

No one is sure precisely when cricket began, but it was sometime in the 1700s. It is often thought of as a genteel game of jolly good sportsmen where just to play is considered the most important aspect. Today's money driven agenda seems a far cry from that. Many also think of violence in sport as a late 20th century phenomenon, but judging by what happened nearly 250 years ago that view is somewhat misplaced.

In October 1776, Essex were about to play Kent at cricket in Tilbury. County names were picked for teams at almost any level as it gave the match an element of prestige. In any event there was no county structure for cricket at that time. The substance of the story that follows is from a Gravesend letter published in the London Chronicle on 31st October 1776.

The Essex and Kent teams had assembled on a pitch at Tilbury Fort. Following the usual pre-match competitive banter, for some reason the Essex team took exception to one of the Kent players and refused to play. This resulted in mayhem. One of the Kent men ran to the guard room and seized a weapon. Upon returning, in the ensuing fracas, the weapon was discharged and a man from the Essex side was shot dead. Immediately the remaining players stormed the guard room. One of the guards was run through with a bayonet and a sergeant, who intervened to try and calm the situation was also killed. Even more appalling was the fact that most of the personnel at the fort were disabled serviceman put on light duties. The Essex men eventually slunk away and the Kent men took to their boats and rowed back across the River Thames to Kent.

In Britain mad King George III was on the throne and America had just made its declaration of independence. The newspaper account remained unchallenged for 200 years when suddenly its authenticity was questioned by cricket buff Leslie Thompson. He surmised that cricket would not have taken place at Tilbury in the first place or as late as October. What may be in his favour is that there are no records of any follow up by the law or further press reports of such a sensational incident.

Settling the Score

On a lighter note, Essex County Cricket Club was not formed for another 100 years, in 1876 at Brentwood. It moved to the present Chelmsford ground in 1966. One hundred and three years later, in 1979, Essex won their first major trophies - the County Championship and the *Benson & Hedges Cup*. Happily there have been no repeats of the match of 1776.

RIGBY'S FOLLIES

Beside the Stour two towers stand,
Relics of a scheme to make Mistley grand.

In 1703 Aubrey de Vere, the 20th Earl of Oxford, died. His estates were divided and six years later a very surprised Edward Rigby, a linen draper in London, learned that he had inherited the village of Mistley and much of the surrounding countryside.

Mistley's two towers and the Swan Fountain, further to the east on the River Stour, are all that remain of a grand scheme to turn Mistley into a spa town. The idea was conceived by Richard Rigby, the grandson of Edward. Work began on the project in 1776. Rigby owned Mistley Hall, a huge mansion, and the family had become exceedingly wealthy. He was also an MP who became Secretary for Ireland. Later he was elevated to Paymaster of the Forces, a cabinet-level post with responsibility for army pay, rations and logistics. It was considered to be one of the most lucrative government positions. The office holder could levy fees on a percentage basis on the monies he disbursed. 1776 was a busy time for the Paymaster. America had declared independence and large numbers of British troops were in America or en-route, backed up by a large naval force.

It was against this background that Rigby embarked on his dream of 'Mistley Spa'. Paymasters before him had left office very rich men. Rigby had no reason to believe he would be different. However there was disquiet in Government circles about financial irregularities within the Paymaster's office. Other cabinet members were jealous. Contracts for building warships mysteriously found their way to the shipyards in Mistley and Rigby was well known as a spendthrift. He regularly held extravagant parties at his mansion. Furthermore he was under a cloud as he had amassed huge gambling debts and also because of his association with the Naze Tower scandal.

This involved clandestine rendezvous between 'actresses' and gentlemen in high places at the then fashionable tea room in the Naze Tower at nearby Walton which was described as the perfect hideaway. The term 'actress' was very loose in all senses of the word and the gentlemen were anything but. But it was all done in the name of theatre and promoting the arts! It might have remained quiet had not one of the actresses, Martha Ray, been shot dead on the steps of Covent Garden Theatre in London by James Hackman, a clergyman.

In October 1781 the American war ended with the defeat of the British Army at Yorktown. Rigby's department was investigated by the House of Commons Commissioners of Public Accounts. Their report urged: *Immediate action to impose check on the money held at any one time by the*

Paymaster whilst in office, and to prevent those leaving office from taking large sums of public money with them.

The system allowed the Paymaster (Rigby) to send the Treasury an estimate of monies needed for the army. The Treasury, without checking, would pay up with no questions asked. This arrangement had operated for years and Rigby had been in the post for fourteen years. On leaving office Paymasters had simply pocketed the surplus balances and kept them until the accounts were finally approved. The previous Paymaster, Henry Fox, benefited from the use of public money for several years after he had left office. It took fifteen years for his accounts to be audited.

Richard Rigby resigned shortly after the Parliamentary commission reported and his funds were frozen. Finance for the Mistley Spa scheme dried up and the project ground to a halt. All that had been built were some lodges, the ornate fountain and a church, the core of which was later demolished, leaving the two still standing towers.

In April 1788, Rigby was somewhat astounded and embarrassed when he was requested to pay back a large sum of money to the public purse. He died in disgrace shortly afterwards, leaving his estate and a host of problems to his sister and then his nephew, Colonel Hale Rigby. Not only did the government want its money back but a long line of personal creditors sought restitution, to say nothing of the vast

expense in the upkeep of Mistley Hall and family houses in London.

Hale Rigby did his best to rectify the financial situation but it was hopeless. The estate and all its problems were in turn inherited by John (the 4th Lord) Rivers, the great grandson of Richard Rigby's sister Martha.

The only solution was liquidation - the village of Mistley would be sold in lots at auction. The first auction began at noon on the 9th of August 1844. The great mansion of Mistley Hall was demolished the same year.

There were further sales in September 1844 and two more in 1845. Everything went under the hammer - wharfs, shipyards, warehouses, farms, the hotel and even the vicarage and rectory. The Rigby connection with Mistley had been severed. The two towers and the fountain are a reminder of what might have been.

AT THE DOCTOR'S POND

'We want an improved method of construction of a boat
That if filled with water will still stay afloat.'

Just north of Great Dunmow town centre, on the Thaxted Road, is the curiously named 'Doctor's Pond'. A plaque on the railings erected during the Golden Jubilee in 2002 states, *legend has it that the name 'Doctor's Pond' is derived from a local doctor's use of the pond for breeding and keeping of leeches used in the medicine of the day.*

However, the pond's main claim to fame is that it is where Lionel Lukin first tested models of lifeboats. This too is mentioned on the plaque, *Lionel Lukin born Great Dunmow 18th May 1742 is famous for inventing the first 'unimerigible' lifeboat in 1784.*

It is somewhat odd that Lukin chose building lifeboats as Great Dunmow is many miles from the coast and Lukin was neither seafarer nor boat builder. Lukin's business was making luxury coaches. He was described as having an inventive mind that liked a challenge. He was also well connected, being acquainted with the Prince Regent and the Prime Minister William Pitt.

By 1785 Lukin had produced a prototype for which he obtained a patent. Further tests of full size boats were carried out on the Thames and in the sea near Ramsgate. His design incorporated water tight compartments and layers of cork to keep the boat afloat. Additional weighting was put on the keel to maintain stability. Lukin's designs were passed on to the Prince Regent but, in spite of encouragement and financial backing, there was little interest from the Navy.

A few of the boats he built were sent to coastal towns for rescue work. In Bamburgh, Northumberland, one was used for many years as a lifeboat. Another was taken to Ramsgate, however this one appeared to have been used for less worthy causes - smuggling. In the same period other lifeboat designers were emerging and Lukin spent much of his time trying to stop his patent being copied.

In the age of sail it was not uncommon for vessels to get into trouble within sight of land in rough weather. In March 1789, the Collier Brig *Adventure* carrying coal was stranded on the Herd Sands, a shoal off Tynemouth a few hundred yards from the shore. Thousands of spectators on land watched helplessly as the ship foundered and the crew were drowned.

Such was the outrage following the tragedy, a reward was offered for the design of a boat "to preserve the lives of seamen, from ships coming ashore".

A local man, Henry Greathead, took up the challenge and produced a design considered a winner. He claimed the credit for the first lifeboat and was duly rewarded by a parliamentary grant of 1,200 guineas.

Meanwhile Lionel Lukin, when not engaged in litigation, had been working on other projects but eventually gave up due to failing eyesight. He retired to Hythe in Kent. On his death he asked for the following inscription to be put on his gravestone:-

"This Lionel Lukin was the first who built a life-boat,
and was the original inventor of that principle of safety,
by which many lives and much property have been preserved from shipwreck;
and he obtained for it the King's patent in the year 1785."

Perhaps he asked for this memorial to set the record straight. It is not known where or when his rival Henry Greathead died or is buried. It is also not known what the other residents of Great Dunmow thought of a grown man playing with model boats at the Doctor's pond.

The National Lifeboat Institution was founded in 1824.

GUNPOWDER'S LOT

The Essex Gunpowder Mills at Waltham Abbey, straddling the River Lea on the county's border with Hertfordshire, were acquired by the Crown in 1787. Prior to that date gunpowder was manufactured by private companies. The Army and the Navy were of the opinion that much of the gunpowder available was substandard. Supply was inconsistent with stocks running out when most needed, as happened during the Dutch wars and the American Revolutionary conflict. Many of the private gunpowder makers had no particular loyalty to the nation, their main interest being making a profit. Following the disaster of the American War and with conflict again looming with the French, the British government decided to nationalise most of the private factories. The Mills at Waltham Abbey were purchased from John Walton for £10,000 and thus The Royal Gunpowder Mills came into being.

Under the watchful eye of Sir William Congreve, Deputy Comptroller of the Royal Laboratory at Woolwich Arsenal, new standards were set and rigorous quality control enforced. Manufacturing processes were upgraded to ensure continuous supply and substantial resources were allocated to research and development. The benchmarks of quality and cost established by the Royal Gunpowder Mills were then imposed on the remaining gunpowder makers in the private sector. For over 200 years the mills remained under Government control with many innovations such as gun cotton, cordite, and the plastic explosive RDX being perfected there.

Although the mills' main purpose was to provide for the military it was also a catalyst in the advancement of explosives for civil use. With the industrial revolution in full swing, gunpowder related products were in great demand for tunnelling, mining and quarrying. During the First World War over 6,000 people worked in the Waltham Abbey factories. Production was dispersed during World War II for fear of enemy bombing. After the conflict was over, work at Waltham Abbey concentrated on research such as rocket fuels and cartridges for firing jet aircraft ejector seats.

However the mills were gradually run down and the Waltham Abbey Mills turned full circle when what remained was privatised and the surplus land sold off to be developed for housing. Currently the Royal Gunpowder Mills are an industrial heritage attraction open to the public at weekends and bank holidays throughout the spring and summer months.

JOHN CONSTABLE'S SCHOOL DAYS

Every day young John would walk to school,
Observing the countryside as an absolute jewel.
Along the banks, across the fields or leafy lanes,
In snow or Summer's heat or wet from the rains.

The River Stour, once the ancient barrier between the Angles and the Saxons, is now the boundary between Essex and Suffolk. From East Bergholt and Flatford on its north bank to Dedham village on its south, the countryside has been immortalised in the paintings of the area's most famous son, John Constable. Constable was born in 1776, in East Bergholt, where his father, Golding Constable, was a prosperous miller and grain merchant. John's parents were keen he should receive a good education but efforts to send him to boarding school were rebuffed. The family then agreed that John should attend nearby at Dedham Grammar School as a day pupil.

Every day for five years John walked the two to three miles from his home, along the river banks and through the countryside, of which he was later to say, *I love every stile, stump and lane….these scenes made me a painter.*

He was already painting and drawing regularly while at school and his headmaster, Dr Thomas Grimwood, once commented, after John's slowness in answering a question, *Oh, John I see that you are in your painting room.*

The school has long since been turned into a private house. It still stands in Dedham High Street and has a plaque over the door commemorating Thomas Grimwood.

On leaving school John worked in the family business. At the age of twenty-three, in 1799, his father made him an allowance to study art in London at the Royal Academy. His approach revolutionised landscape painting yet in spite of this he was not elected a full member of the academy for another thirty years.

John Constable and his wife Maria came to stay in Leigh-on-Sea where he thought the air would be good for Maria's health. It was while staying at the house of his Uncle Thomas, sadly demolished in 1952, that he made sketches for his famous paintings of Hadleigh Castle. One of these may be seen in the Tate Britain gallery in London.

His paintings of the Stour valley, particularly of Dedham Vale, Dedham Mill, Flatford Mill, The Hay Wain and Willy Lott's Cottage, are now internationally recognised throughout the art world. This group depicts scenes that are still recognisable today. The Dedham Vale area is visited annually by thousands of tourists anxious to see for themselves the countryside he made so famous.

As his fame and reputation grew in the late nineteenth century this area of the Essex and Suffolk border became known as 'Constable Country'.

WATERWAY TO CHELMSFORD

Maldon was a big port, Chelmsford a small town.
Maldon didn't want a canal; afraid of trade going down.

The idea of making the river Chelmer navigable was first mooted in 1677. It gained little support even though many of Chelmsford's needs came from the major port of Maldon involving lengthy, and costly, transport by pack mules or wagon and horses. In 1733 the sum of £9,355 for making the Chelmer navigable was considered too much and another estimate 30 years later of £13,000 was also rejected. The people of Maldon were afraid of losing valuable port dues and trading monopolies.

In 1793 however a new Act of Parliament approved a scheme, bypassing Maldon, for a canal from Heybridge Basin terminating at Springfield. In July the same year, *The Company of Proprietors of the Chelmer and Blackwater Navigation Limited*, held its first meeting. In October John Rennie was appointed Director and Richard Coats day to day manager. They had worked together on the Ipswich to Stowmarket canal. Using the same team of experienced Suffolk navies, the Chelmer Navigation was completed in record time to open fully in 1797.

The canal was a great success. Over a length of nearly fourteen miles there were twelve locks which allowed passage for heavy barges and lighters. In its busiest year, 1842, the canal carried sixty thousand tons of cargo. Sawmills, lime kilns, iron foundries, stone masons and coal merchants were just some of the industries that sprang up around the Springfield basin terminal.

In Chelmsford the first inland gasworks in Britain was built using coal brought by barge in 25 ton loads. A little downstream from Hoe Mill, Britain's first sugar refinery was established in 1832. The aptly named 'Paper Mill' located at North Hill, Little Baddow, was the first producer of paper in Essex and gave its name to 'Paper Mill Lock' which was later to become the headquarters of the Proprietors of C&BN (Chelmer and Blackwater Navigation) Ltd. Paper Mill Lock is the half way point on the canal between Heybridge and Chelmsford and was where bargees could find overnight accommodation.

In 1843 the Eastern Counties London to Colchester Railway, built with materials mostly barged up from Heybridge, was completed. From then on there was a steady decline in traffic using the canal. Horse drawn barges were replaced with motorised vessels in 1960 but 1972 saw the last commercial cargo on the canal. However the building of this navigable waterway was a major boost in the development of Chelmsford from a small market town to the County Town (now City) that it is today.

In 1978 the Navigation Company had sold all of its lighters and commissioned *The Victoria*, a purpose built vessel 58ft long by 12' 6" wide and licensed to carry 48 passengers. This vessel may still be chartered for pleasure cruises and corporate functions and operates from Paper Mill lock.

The canal is still owned by the same company although it is now managed on their behalf by the Inland Waterways Association. The Chelmer Canal Trust Limited, a registered charity, is a voluntary group who also contribute to the upkeep of the canal and its environs. Fishermen, canoeists and boating enthusiasts all use the canal and the towpath may be walked for the fourteen miles of waterway from Chelmsford all the way to Heybridge basin.

HARVEY'S SEA FENCIBLES

You are the First Sea Fencibles of Essex, every man.
Each and every one of you," Harvey barked most intense.
"Are our eyes and ears, essential for our coastal defence.

The Essex Sea Fencibles: Probably the least known unit in the history of Britain's defences.

HMS Temeraire: A ship of war launched in 1798, built from oak cut in Hainault Forest, made famous in a painting by JMW Turner.

The Battle of Trafalgar 1805: England's most celebrated naval victory.

These three subjects have a common link, Sir Eliab Harvey of Rolls Park, Chigwell. As the 18th century closed Britain was again embroiled in war with France. The threat of a seaborne invasion was very real. This led to the creation of a coastal defence force known as the Sea Fencibles. The entire English coast facing the European mainland was covered by the scheme, as was Lands End and the whole shoreline up as far as Bristol.

The Sea Fencibles were a nautical Home Guard manned by part-time volunteers. Essex Sea Fencibles' zone began in Leigh-on-Sea in the south of the county and ran around the Essex shoreline to Harwich. The force comprised about 1,500 men divided into small units, each serving their own community.

Most of the volunteers lived in shacks on the coast and eked out a living from fishing and bait digging. One of the great advantages of joining the Sea Fencibles was that it exempted its members from being impressed into the navy. The fear of the navy's strong armed press gangs turning up unannounced was very real.

Eliab Harvey's background couldn't have been more different from that of the average Sea Fencible. He was born into a privileged family at the huge Rolls Park estate which originally dominated much of Chigwell. Educated at Westminster and Harrow, he enrolled in the navy whilst still a pupil. When his elder brother William died suddenly, Eliab, just 21, inherited the estate plus a vast fortune.

The next year Eliab Harvey became MP for Maldon. Parliamentary duties didn't interrupt his naval career but after four years he resigned the seat. By the age of 35 he was in command of the *Valiant*, a 74-gun ship of the line, and saw action in the West Indies. Unfortunately Eliab contracted dengue fever in Jamaica which forced him to return home in late 1798.

Although poorly, Harvey begged the Admiralty to find him something to do.

As going back to sea was out of the question, their ingenious solution was to offer him a part-time job as Captain of the Essex Sea Fencibles. For Harvey this arrangement was ideal. He could divide his time between recuperating at home in Chigwell and when required on field duties could stay in one of many comfortable lodgings scattered around the Essex coast. Ideal it may have seemed but this command offered Harvey no excitement. The threatened invasion never materialised. The Fencibles were never called out in defence of the realm nor took part in any meaningful action. It was also apparent that having charge of a bunch of part-timers was quite different to life in the navy. The iron discipline that ruled a 'Man-o-War' could not be enforced on civilian volunteers.

Many of the Fencibles who lived around the Rivers Crouch and Blackwater were probably involved in smuggling in one form or another. They benefited enormously from the Navy's distribution of weapons and offers of sea combat and signals training. Furthermore volunteers were paid one shilling a day when they attended!

In 1803, Harvey having left the Fencibles was appointed Captain of the *Temeraire*. When he later joined Nelson at the battle of Trafalgar, the *Temeraire* helped save Nelson's ship the *Victory*, which was in danger of being overwhelmed by the French ship *Redoubtable*. Today the *Victory* is preserved as a monument in Portsmouth's Royal Naval Dockyard.

The *Temeraire* survived until 1838 and would have been completely forgotten had it not been for the painter J.M.W. Turner. After witnessing the ship being towed up the Thames by a steam tug to be broken up, he produced *The Fighting Temeraire*, one of the nation's most famous paintings.

As for Eliab Harvey, he was promoted to Rear Admiral. Shortly afterwards he was dismissed from active service. He was accused of insulting his commander before the attack on Basque Roads in the Bay of Biscay. Harvey returned to his Rolls Park estate, his wife Louisa, their nine children and Parliament. He was still a hero to many and the public outcry at his treatment by the admiralty led to his reinstatement as a Rear Admiral.

Harvey was eventually promoted to full Admiral although he never went to sea again. With the threat of invasion over, the Essex Sea Fencibles faded into obscurity and was disbanded in 1810.

Harvey's Sea Fencibles reporting for duty

TIMELINE

ESSEX EVENT	AD	NATIONAL or INTERNATIONAL EVENT
Eliab Harvey commands Temeraire	1805	*Battle of Trafalgar*
	1812	*British PM Spenser Percival is assassinated in Parliament*
Excavation of Bartlow Hills starts	1815	*Battle of Waterloo*
Hard Apple arrested at sea	1820	*Birth of Florence Nightingales*
John Constable paints Hadleigh Castle	1829	*Birth of Geronimo, Apache leader*
Machine breaking in Lt. Clacton	1831	*Belgium become independent*
David Livingston get lost in Ongar	1838	*Public Record Office established.*
Essex gets it first Chief Constable	1840	*Postage stamps (Penny Black) issued*
Plum Puddings eaten at Romford Workhouse on Christmas day	1841	*Britain claims Hong Kong*
HMS Warrior launched in Bow Creek	1860	*Abraham Lincoln elected US President*
Coalhouse Fort completed	1874	*Disraeli becomes Prime Minister*
Essex County Cricket Club formed	1876	*Wyatt Earp arrives in Dodge City*
Essex Earthquake	1884	*General Gordon besieged in Khartoum*
A.C. Wilkin founds Tiptree Jam	1885	*Statue of Liberty arrives in USA*
Southend Iron Pier opens	1889	*Moulin Rouge cabaret opens in Paris*
Creation of Kynocktown	1890	*Death of Vincent van Gough*
Sally Army Colony opens in Hadleigh	1891	*Edison patents movie camera*
Courtaulds gets the rights to 'Viscose'	1904	*Panama Canal Started*
Morris Dancing starts in Thaxted	1911	*Hiram Bingham finds Machu Picchu*
Death of Captain Oats	1912	*Titanic sinks on maiden voyage*
Zeppelin L33 crashes at Peldon	1916	*Battle of the Somme*
Bertram the Clown opens in Clacton	1922	*Stalin become leader of Soviet Union*
Two churches at Willingale combine	1929	*Wall Street crash*
Bata shoe factory opens in Tilbury	1933	*Hitler appointed German Chancellor*
Little Ships rescue troops from France	1940	*Winston Churchill becomes PM*
Essex floods	1953	*Everest first climbed*
Bradwell's Magnox opens	1962	*Cuban Missile Crisis*
GLC formed, Essex borders changed	1965	*Rhodesia declares UDI*
Chelmer Navigation closed to freight	1972	*Bloody Sunday in Northern Ireland*
Space Shuttle lands at Stansted	1983	*Margaret Thatcher wins second term*
Elizabeth Fry the face of £5.00 note	1992	*English Premier League formed*
Death of Sir Alf Ramsay	1999	*Welsh assembly opens in Cardiff*
Bradwell Magnox closes	2002	*Euro Notes and coins introduced*
Olympic Mountain Biking in Hadleigh	2012	*Diamond Jubilee of Queen Elizabeth II*

GRAVE DIGGERS

We rushed out to see what was going on
And saw the whole church roof had gone.

Market day was held in Chelmsford every week outside the Shire Hall. Friday 17th January 1800 was a cold blustery day. Merchants from all over Essex had come to display their wares. All things were normal, all considered. Once again the country was at war the French and the threat to the nation this time seemed severe. Napoleon, now master of most of Europe, had Britain firmly in his sights. Invasion fears were rife and the garrison stationed in Chelmsford outnumbered the town's population by nearly two to one.

In the early afternoon traders began to pack up before dusk fell. Close by, inside St Mary's Parish Church, workmen were chipping away around the stone pillars on the south arcade that held up the church roof. A vault was to be opened. The men were working as fast as they could. An internment was to be held early in the following week and they were not keen on working in a dark church when night had fallen.

By six in the evening all was quiet in the market place. Close by a dozen inns and taverns were doing a roaring trade - their doors pulled tight shut to keep out the winter cold. The raucous din generated within could not be heard in the churchyard. The quiet in the town centre was interrupted when the bells on the church tower chimed nine. Silence returned. Suddenly a resounding crash pierced the night air followed by an avalanche of breaking glass and snapping timbers. A chorus of madly barking dogs broke out. Horses whinnied and wildly kicked at their stable doors in the brewery on Duke Street.

The merriment in the inns halted abruptly. The occupants nervously edged towards the door to peer out. In the pitch dark, and in the absence of street lighting, it was difficult to see anything. The air was thick with dust. Something terrible had happened. With daylight the next morning a scene of utter devastation revealed itself in the church grounds. The columns of the south arcade had collapsed, bringing down the roof and parts of the north and south aisle. In the process the pews and the lower galleries had been smashed, together with many icons and works of art. A great sheet of lead hung precariously over the organ that so far had remained miraculously undamaged.

Everything was coated in a thick layer of dust. *The Essex Chronicle* summed it up - "this stupendous ruin forms a scene of such awful and magnificent grandeur, words are inadequate to describe".

Crowds of sightseers arrived and a young artist Samuel Nathan Summers, arrived with his stool, palette, paints and easel to capture the scene. Within a week the *Chronicle* was carrying advertisements for engraved copies of his paintings which sold out rapidly.

A parish meeting was urgently convened. It immediately authorized work to begin in shoring up the shattered church and retrieving the precious 'Hancock' organ. Within six months a Parliamentary bill had been passed enabling finance for re-building to go ahead. Three and half years later, on Sunday 18th September 1803, the newly restored church held its first service. It is remarkable how quickly the church was rebuilt.

The 'Parish Church' became a Cathedral in 1914 when the Diocese of Chelmsford was created. Chelmsford Cathedral still holds one of the original 1801 bills for decoration – the repainting of the replacement Georgian gothic ceiling in Naples yellow - some 13 guineas. The roof collapse was blamed on the careless 'grave diggers' working in the church that Friday afternoon. There are no records of what became of the men. They may even have been recruited to help clear the damage or ironically even employed on the church rebuilding.

THE FIVE POUND NOTE

Told of the horrors of women's prison life,
Elizabeth Fry, a good Quaker wife,
Went to see the women in Newgate jail
Crammed thirty to a cell with no hope of bail.

For 25 years, between 1992 and 2017, Elizabeth Fry adorned the £5 note. She was chosen in recognition of her work in prison reform.

Elizabeth was born in Norwich in 1780 to wealthy, middle class Quakers, John and Catherine Gurney. In 1800 she married Joseph Fry, the son of a successful Essex merchant family who were also Quakers, and came to live in the Fry family home in Plashet Park, in East Ham which is today part of the London Borough of Newham.

In 1813, Elizabeth Fry, who was now a Quaker preacher and had already given birth to eight children, made her first visit to Newgate Prison*. As a child in Norwich, Elizabeth had accompanied her mother collecting clothes for the poor and visiting the sick. None of those experiences prepared her for the horrors of Newgate. She found women, and their children, living thirty to a cell in such squalor, filth and deprivation that she resolved to devote her energies to improving their lot.

During the next three years she organised friends to collect clothing for the inmates and by 1816 she had become a frequent visitor. She formed the 'Association for the Improvement of the Female Prisoners in Newgate'. This group established a school, with a teacher elected from the inmates, a chapel and regular bible readings. They organised a system of supervision by matrons and monitors and provided materials for compulsory sewing duties where the women could make items to sell.

Fry was opposed to the death penalty and campaigned vigorously for its abolition. At that time there were over two hundred offences, including the passing of forged notes and stealing clothing, which carried the death penalty. Through her brother-in-law, Thomas Fowell Buxton, the MP for Weymouth, she was invited to address the House of Commons. Whilst impressed with her charitable work, the majority of MPs believed that her views on capital punishment were misplaced. She pleaded with the Home Secretary, Lord Sidmouth, for the lives of two women condemned for forgery. He would not budge, warning Fry that her dangerous ideas would, "remove the dread of punishment in the criminal classes".

She continued the campaign, visiting prisons throughout the country, though prisons were not her only targets for reform. After seeing convicts being taken to the ships for transportation, in open carts with hand and leg shackles, she was successful in changing the way they were treated. She arranged for them to be taken in closed carriages to protect them from the missiles of the mob and the shackles were removed. Visiting the convict ships became another regular duty for one of Fry's committees. Robert Peel, who succeeded Lord Sidmouth, and was more sympathetic, allowed many 'Fry inspired' improvements to be included in his '1823 Gaols Act'.

Queen Victoria (nearly forty years younger than Fry) was a great admirer of her charitable work and wrote in her journal of Fry as, "a very superior person". Her influence was not confined to England. Towards the end of her life she visited many of the royal families of Europe to explain her work. In fact the King of Prussia dined with her on a visit to the Fry family home.

Elizabeth Fry died on 12 October 1845 after a short illness. Fry's popularity may perhaps be measured by the fact that, although Quakers do not have funeral services, over one thousand people stood in silence as she was buried at 'The Society of Friends' graveyard in Barking.

Elizabeth Fry's days on the five pound came to an end in 2017. An Essex connection will remain though as the new plasticised note carries the image of former Prime Minister, war time leader and Essex Member of Parliament for Wanstead and Woodford, Sir Winston Churchill.

* Newgate Prison closed in May 1902. The site was cleared for the new Central Criminal Court(Old Bailey) which opened in 1907. Most of the remaining women prisoners were transferred to Holloway.

THE WATERLOO RECTOR

The church of Saint Mary the Virgin, the Parish Church of Little Thurrock, is located on the north bank of the Thames in Dock Road. The church was built around 1170 and is a 'Grade II Star Listed Building'. It contains the tomb of one of the few clergymen who fought under the Duke of Wellington at the Battle of Waterloo. The remains of Reverend Edward Bowlby, the 52nd rector, are interred below the sanctuary. On leaving school, Edward followed his brother Peter into the army and served with the King's Own 4th Regiment of Foot.

At 6pm, on 18th June 1815, the day of the Battle of Waterloo, 20 year old Lieutenant Edward Bowlby went into action just to the north-east of the farm of La Haye Sante. The farm had just fallen to Napoleon's forces. During the campaign the 4th Regiment suffered the loss of 12 men killed and 122 wounded.

On returning to England Edward Bowlby resigned his commission and entered Jesus College, Cambridge, graduating with a BA in theology in 1822. In 1838 he was appointed Rector of St Mary's, Little Thurrock, where he remained for 22 years. A very generous man, he funded several additions to the rectory, a new vestry on the south side of the church and ornaments for the pulpit. He died in office on 25th June 1860 at the age 65. His successor was the Reverend E. Davis.

The Battle of Waterloo was a decisive battle in European history which finally vanquished Napoleon's ambitions to rule Europe. Its connection to Thurrock through the part played by the Rector of Little Thurrock parish church may not have been realised had it not been for a couple of coincidences. In August 2014, in the course of First World War research, a newspaper article in the *Southend Telegraph* of July 1915, was discovered. It carried a brief report on Lieutenant Bowlbys' Waterloo connection with Little Thurrock 100 years earlier. Then in June 2015 during a refurbishment of St Mary's church the carpet behind the sanctuary was lifted revealing the grave of Edward Bowlby which none of the current church community had realised was there.

ONCE THERE WERE SEVEN

Their Roman age secrets remained unseen
Until excavated in eighteen fifteen'.

There are three remaining Bartlow 'Hills', lying just outside Ashdon in the north of the county. They were once part of the largest group of Roman barrows or burial mounds in Northern Europe. Their steep conical shape is typical of the Roman era. Originally seven were 'built' and in the open countryside they looked like a range of small hills.

For centuries the hills lay undisturbed, merely idle curiosities for locals. In the 1700s, an awakening of interest in field archaeology led to the opening of Roman and Saxon burial mounds. As treasures were revealed in some mounds, the aspirations of those working for the benefit of science and history were ruthlessly pushed aside by others who saw financial gain.

Barrow digging became a sport that grew rapidly, often patronised by local squires wanting to furnish their houses with decorative relics. Barrow diggers roamed the land indiscriminately digging up whatever they could find. Very often the methods used were shocking and more was destroyed in opening the site than was recovered. Rarely were any accurate records kept of what was found.

The Bartlow site came to the attention of the diggers in 1815, the year of the Battle of Waterloo, and was a typical example of the cavalier attitude prevalent at that time. Mr Busic Harwood, a retired Cambridge physician, turned up with a large party of men armed with rudimentary tools and began excavations. He is quoted as saying 'my intention is to provide work for the unemployed'. The party dug from the apex downwards. Exactly what Harwood and his men found is not known since the content unearthed simply disappeared without being recorded. It is suspected that all the 'loot' was shared out amongst the diggers who dispersed after the job was done.

Later excavations took place in April 1832, supervised by the historian John Gage of the Society of Antiquities. These digs were conducted in a much more scientific manner and items recovered were logged and carefully stored. Nevertheless, the opening of the remaining barrows took place in a carnival like atmosphere. The list of attendees to the April dig read like a 'Who's Who' of the locality.

A contemporary report lists the attendance of Lord Maynard (later Viscount Maynard), the land owner, Lord Braybrooke, a neighbour,

Professor Sedgewick, the Reverends Whelwell and Lodge, the Rectors of Ashdon and Bartlow respectively and several ladies and gentlemen from the locality together with their families, servants and workmen all dressed in their best.

The dig produced a number of relics, especially glass and china urns, a bronze lamp and the remains of burial caskets. After cataloguing they were removed for safekeeping to Easton Lodge in Dunmow, the family home of Lord Maynard. The barrows, now empty, were then left in peace although four of the smaller mounds were flattened during the construction of the Colchester and Stour Valley Railway in 1846.

A year later disaster struck when Easton Lodge caught fire and burnt to the ground, incinerating everything within. John Gage's dig had cleared up one mystery though. Previously it had been suspected that the 'Bartlow Hills' were burial mounds for Danish soldiers who died fighting the Anglo Saxons. Careful analysis by Gage identified the mounds as being Roman.

In 1978, overgrown and neglected, the hills were taken into care by Essex County Council. They now lie just over the border from Essex in Cambridgeshire following a minor boundary change in 1990. A number of papers relating to the site excavation can be found in Saffron Walden Library and there are a few artefacts in Saffron Walden Museum.

HARD APPLE

William Blyth was a smuggler nicknamed 'Hard Apple'
With whom the Revenue for years tried to grapple.

Paglesham is one of the county's oldest fishing villages and William Blyth one of the most colourful characters from its past. Born in 1753, known to all as 'Hard Apple', he grew up to become a pillar of the community. During his 74 years he was the village grocer, a parish councillor, churchwarden, constable and even magistrate, as well as being a successful oysterman. His marriage to Mary Dowsett linked his own large family to William Dowsett, fellow oysterman and notorious smuggler.

Paglesham oysters were renowned for their quality and a good living was to be made from farming them. However lucrative though, it could not come close to the profits to be made from smuggling. Blyth and Dowsett, along with the Pagelsham families of the Embersons and the Wisemans, under cover of exporting oysters to the continent, made their village the smuggling capital of the East Coast.

Just how William Blyth came by the name of 'Hard Apple' is not known though it is said that he was a man who feared nothing and lived life to the full and that drink had no effect on him. Although he had many encounters with customs officers, according to their records he was never actually charged with anything.

Once when caught, his illicit cargo was taken aboard a revenue cutter. Blyth is then reputed to have begun drinking with the crew until they were drunk and incapable. He then transferred his cargo back to his own boat, plus contraband previously confiscated from other boats, thus showing a double profit on the day.

On another occasion he was arrested at sea and clapped in irons by the customs officer of Leigh, John Loten. When the revenue cutter ran aground on the Goodwin Sands Loten pleaded with Blyth to use his knowledge of the area to help them. Blyth is reputed to have answered, "I might as well drown as be hanged," but with the prospect of the vessel breaking up, in return for his freedom, he was persuaded to use his expertise to get them back to safe waters.

His exploits on land were just as outrageous. The nickname of 'Hard Apple' may well have come from his reputation for hard drinking. William Blyth died in 1830 and is buried in St Peter's Churchyard near 'The Punch Bowl', the scene of much of his legendary drinking.

CAPTAIN SWING

All the protesters long remember,
that eighth of December.
a mob did arise
and took the authorities quite by surprise.

The Napoleonic wars were over. Many soldiers and sailors had returned home from years of service overseas. Times were hard and there was little in the way of civilian employment. History was seen to be repeating itself, whereby depression followed a great military victory. At the same time the industrial revolution was gathering pace which threatened the livelihoods of the already low paid agricultural workers. There was no obvious spark, just hearsay and rumour, but suddenly in 1830 much of rural southeast England was engulfed in a great wave of machine breaking as a protest.

On 7th December a mob of 150 ran riot in Great Clacton. Two days later a similar sized group, fuelled by drink, assembled in the dead of night in Little Clacton with the express purpose of seeking out and destroying a thrashing machine kept in a locked barn there.

The leader of the rioters was a so called 'Captain Swing' who supposedly took his name from the 'swing' or moving part of the flail used to thrash the grain. The rioters, in turn, were collectively referred to as Swing Rioters. After the protest died down, the authorities moved swiftly and showed little mercy in pursuing the ring leaders and their associates. Fifty Essex men from Clacton were charged with a variety of offences. Nationally some 2,000 men and women were convicted and over 500 were transported to Van Diemen's Land (now Tasmania, Australia) to serve between 5 and 14 year terms.

One local man, Benjamin Hackshall, made a futile attempt to escape arrest, first by hiding up a neighbour's chimney for days, then fleeing to London. However he was apprehended on New Year's Day. Luckily for him he escaped transportation. After having served a relatively short spell in Chelmsford jail, he returned to his family in Little Clacton. Hackshall then became a minor celebrity by composing a popular ballad, which gave a romantic account of the riots.

Five years later, in February 1835, 200 of those convicted and transported received free pardons, although most chose to stay in Australia.

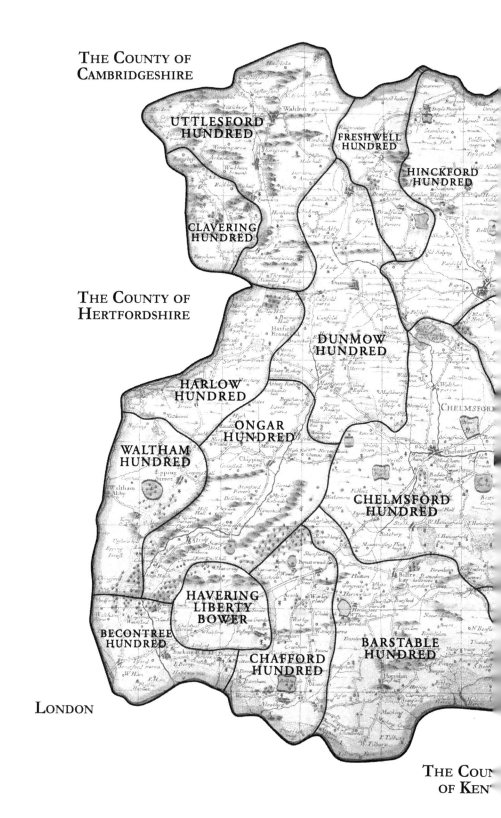

THE COUNTY OF
CAMBRIDGESHIRE

THE COUNTY OF
HERTFORDSHIRE

UTTLESFORD
HUNDRED

FRESHWELL
HUNDRED

HINCKFORD
HUNDRED

CLAVERING
HUNDRED

DUNMOW
HUNDRED

HARLOW
HUNDRED

ONGAR
HUNDRED

WALTHAM
HUNDRED

CHELMSFORD
HUNDRED

HAVERING
LIBERTY
BOWER

BECONTREE
HUNDRED

CHAFFORD
HUNDRED

BARSTABLE
HUNDRED

LONDON

THE COUNTY
OF KENT

The Hundreds
of Essex

The County of
Suffolk

LEXDEN HUNDRED

TENDRING
HUNDRED

THAM
IDRED

WINSTRED
HUNDRED

THURSTABLE
HUNDRED

DENGY HUNDRED

THE NORTH SEA

ROCHFORD HUNDRED

THE RIVER THAMES

The WITHAM FIRES

In three interrogations, three times James confessed
Each one contradicting the one that he'd made last.
No evidence was found; but something had to be done.
So James was sent to prison and still the fires went on,
The jury found him guilty, 'give him mercy' they all cried.
'The Judge, wanting an example set, said; 'mercy is denied!'

In the evening of 5th of November 1828 two fires broke out in Witham. Initially thought to be accidents, the result of fireworks from Guy Fawkes celebrations, investigations showed that they were deliberately started. When two more fires occurred in December a sense of alarm spread through the town, probably exacerbated by memories of earlier rioting and arson throughout East Anglia and particularly in north Essex. A reward of £200, for information leading to the apprehension of the culprit, was offered by the Member of Parliament, Mr. Western. An association for 'the Protection of Life and Property against Fire' was formed. A watch system was set up and a new fire-engine purchased. The local magistrates interviewed several suspects; all were released. In the December Petty Sessions ten new Special Constables from Witham were sworn in. (There was no Essex police force until 1840.)

In January 1829 there was a further spate of fires in north Essex and on 19th and 20th February there were two more fires in Witham, the first in a hay-stack belonging to William Whale, an innkeeper, and the second in William Green's barn at Oliver's Farm. Five days later James Cook, a cow boy who lived over the brewhouse at Oliver's Farm, was interrogated about the fire. At sixteen years old he was the oldest of the six children of a widow, Dorcas Cook. Her husband had died in 1827 and she and her five children were living on poor relief.

On the 2nd of March there was yet another fire in Witham and two days later William Luard, the Magistrate, and Revd. John Newman sent James Cook to the new convict gaol at Chelmsford to await trial for causing the fire at Oliver's Farm. While he was in custody, on 7th March, another fire destroyed an outhouse belonging to William Grimwood. Despite this his prosecution continued.

On three occasions under interrogation James Cook 'confessed', each confession contradicting the others, yet he was still sent for trial. On the 12th of March at the Lent Assizes, at the Shire Hall in Chelmsford, the jury returned a verdict of guilty but recommended mercy, as did William Green his prosecutor. The judge, Mr. Justice Alexander, pronounced the death sentence as was expected. It was normal for this to be a formality and immediate afterwards a reprieve announced with the sentence commuted to imprisonment or transportation. On this occasion the judge, no doubt mindful of the waves of arson, rioting and machine breaking in the county, said he felt that 'a severe example' was necessary to 'put a stop to such national calamities', and that James Cook should therefore be hanged.

On 18th and 19th of March, Luard, the magistrate, wrote to Robert Peel the Home Secretary and to Queen Victoria, via the Home Office, asking for a Royal Pardon. He received the reply from J. M. Phillips, the under-secretary at the Home Office, that it would be reckless to pardon Cook, in view of his confessions.

So James Cook was hanged on 27th March outside Chelmsford gaol in front of a great crowd. Hanging was quite a rare occurrence at this time; there were no others in Essex in 1829. There was widespread anger against the judge and the sentence which was considered a cruel act of injustice. However, the fires continued and on the 18th of April an apprentice tailor, Edmund Potto, was interrogated and committed to gaol. He was eventually tried on eight counts of arson and connected offences. He pleaded insanity but was found guilty on one count and sentenced to transportation. After his arrest there were no more fires.

The last execution at Chelmsford's Springfield Prison, on November 4th 1914, was that of Charles Fremd who was convicted of murdering his wife. He was also, at 71, the oldest man to be hanged in Britain. A German born grocer from Leytonstone, Fremd was found beside his wife in bed. She had had her throat cut and he was laid beside her with only a minor self inflicted wound to his throat. He had left a note which read; "Her first husband made off with himself I cannot stand it any longer. God forgive me. Her temper done it".

The execution was carried out by John Ellis; it was his last job as public executioner at Springfield and there were no further executions carried out there.

Shortly afterwards the prison was taken over by the army as a military goal although it reverted to civilian use in 1931.

SAD DAYS AT HIGH BEECH

My sleep is restless and I feel my power ebbs away.
The forest trees hem me in and keep me at bay.

Alfred, Lord Tennyson, is one of England's most celebrated poets. Born in 1809, on his death at 81 he was buried in poets' corner at Westminster Abbey. His best remembered poem *The Charge of the Light Brigade* was published in 1855 as a memorial to the suicidal charge of the British light cavalry at the Battle of Balaclava in the Crimean War a year earlier.

Tennyson was twenty when he won the Chancellor's Gold Medal at Trinity College Cambridge. He left Cambridge, without taking his degree, in 1831 on the death of his father. In 1833 Tennyson published his second book of poetry. Some critics of the day revelled in the severity of their critical reviews. This hurt Tennyson badly, so much so that he published nothing further for nine years although he continued to write. In the same year he was traumatized by the sudden death of his friend Arthur Hallam at the age of 22.

In 1837 Tennyson became engaged to his childhood sweetheart, Emily Sellwood. Soon after, the Tennysons moved to High Beech House on the edge of Epping Forrest, while Emily was left in Lincolnshire. Tennyson spent three years at High Beech with his mother, generally feeling sorry for himself. He wrote often to Emily saying how he missed her and how awful life was at High Beech. Emotionally and financially these were difficult years for Tennyson. He claimed he could not even afford the train fare to visit Emily. Suffering from depression, he stayed for two weeks as a guest in Dr. Matthew Allen's High Beech Asylum. He reported that mad people were *the most agreeable and most reasonable persons he had me*t. Tennyson would later regret the acquaintance of Dr. Allen. Whilst apparently not having money for a train fare he managed to invest his family's money in a woodcarving scheme of the doctor's and lost everything. As a consequence plans to marry Emily were postponed again.

If High Beech and Epping Forest provided a setting to match Tennyson's mood it was a productive one. It was here that he began writing his epic poem *In Memoriam*, a tribute to his late friend Arthur Hallam. It took him 17 years to write. Within two years of leaving Essex for Tunbridge Wells, in 1840, he published two volumes of poems, which met with immediate success.

This was the beginning of real recognition for Tennyson. In 1850 he married Emily, was created Poet Laureate and published *In Memoriam*, to universal acclaim. The next forty years produced a body of work that has made him the second most frequently quoted writer after Shakespeare. It would appear that, for all the sadness Tennyson felt in Essex, his stay there was a significant turning point on his road to greatness.

LOST IN ONGAR

At Stanford Rivers the fog had grown thicker
He climbed a lamppost to see which road would be quicker

At the age of 27, the famous explorer and missionary Doctor David Livingstone went to Africa. He travelled down the great Zambezi River to discover 'The Smoke that Thunders,' which he renamed Victoria Falls after the then Queen. Two years before his death, after a long search, the journalist Henry Morgan Stanley met Livingstone in 1871 with the famous phrase, *Doctor Livingstone I presume*. During his 30 years in Africa Livingstone crossed the continent from the Atlantic to the Indian Ocean, in the process walking some 5,000 miles. Although he died in Africa, his body was brought to England to be interred in Westminster Abbey.

A self-educated Scot from Blantyre, Livingstone trained as a doctor in Glasgow. In 1838 he was accepted as a probationer by the London Missionary Society. He was then sent to study under the Rev. Richard Cecil in Chipping Ongar. He lodged with other students in what are now called the 'Livingstone Cottages' in Ongar High Street. During that time his colleague and fellow probationer Joseph Moore recorded an incident which, in view of his future achievements, was surprising to say the least. One November day David Livingstone set off on foot to London to visit a sick relative, a round trip of some fifty miles. Fellow students marvelled at the energy and drive that would be needed to walk this distance. Later in the day Dr Livingstone returned via Edmonton. There is a story that he stopped to render assistance to a lady who had fallen off her horse but this cannot be verified.

However, with night falling and a thick fog descending, the doctor lost his way at Stanford Rivers not far from Ongar. Naturally by this time he felt weary and footsore. After some time walking round in circles he managed to find a lampost on which he climbed and managed to get his bearings. Eventually, with the clock striking 12 midnight, David

Livingstone made it back, much to the relief of his fellow students. Nevertheless he was ribbed mercilessly in the following days.

Was the experience of getting lost on a 50-mile walk in Essex adequate preparation for a 5,000-mile walk across uncharted Africa? We shall never know.

CHRISTMAS DAY IN THE WORKHOUSE.

At Romford Union Workhouse then
Imagine the furore
When on Christmas day plum puddings
Were given to the poor.

Prior to 1834 each parish had to take care of its poor. Romford was no exception and the amount of the poor rate was always a bone of contention for those that paid it. For the workhouse inmates, their Christmas diet was like any other day, the extra expense of seasonal fare being considered unacceptable.

The Romford Poor Law Union, formed in 1836, brought the poor of ten parishes; Barking, Cranham, Dagenham, Hornchurch, Havering-atte-Bower, Rainham, Romford, Upminster, Great Warley and Wennington, under the responsibility of one Board of Guardians. With the new organisation came some enlightened thinking. Within three years the board had bought a five acre site at Oldchurch and built a 'state of the art' new workhouse with a capacity for 450 people. The 'enlightened thinking', to some of the public, may have been a step too far when, in 1841, there appeared a report in the *Essex Standard* stating that, 'On Christmas day, the 400 inmates had been given 240 plum puddings, with a total weight of 600 lbs'.

The Guardians withstood the criticism of wasting ratepayers' money and the practice of allowing inmates to celebrate Christmas like this was established for future years.

The workhouse, of necessity, had its own infirmary. In time it came to treat not only the residents but also the poor generally. This aspect of its work gathered such a reputation that, in 1893, a hospital was added. Experience gained by the staff during and after the Great War led to its recognition as a respected medical institution. In 1924 the hospital was expanded becoming bigger than the workhouse itself.

The Poor Law Union was dissolved in 1930, the institution being taken over by Essex County Council. In 1935 the Public Health Committee took over responsibility for Oldchurch Hospital. It continued to expand over the next sixty years to become a major regional hospital.

In the year 2000 the hospital, having outgrown the piecemeal additions to the old Victorian buildings, was closed. It was replaced by the new, state of the art; Queens Hospital built just a short walk away. At the time of writing Oldchurch Hospital, with the exception of the old nurses' accommodation block has been demolished and is being redeveloped for housing.

In 2013 negotiations began for the Oasis learning Academy, to open a primary Free School in the nurses' accommodation block, which is currently planned to open in 2016. It is not known how much of the original building will be retained.

HOCKLEY SPA

For London, Essex waters had become all the rage
All digestive problems they were said to assuage.

The belief that taking mineral waters or bathing in spa waters was a cure for all sorts of human ailments has been around for hundreds of years. However life style remedies tend to go round in circles. What is fashionable today is suddenly out of favour tomorrow. In spite of this there has been no end of candidates willing to try their luck and risk all their money, or someone else's, in spa ventures.

The great spa towns in England such as Bath, Buxton and Harrogate have all had their ups and downs. As we have shown earlier (see page 82) Richard Rigby, a minister of the crown, spent much of his own fortune, and considerable amounts of taxpayer's money, on a private project to create a spa town in Mistley on the River Stour. It ended in financial disaster and disgrace for Rigby.

In the 1830s the small village of Hockley became the site of a less ambitious spa project. Robert and Leticia Clay moved to Hockley from Cheltenham (another spa town) in the hope that the fresh Essex country air would relieve Mrs Clay's persistent asthmatic cough. Within a short time Mrs Clay's condition had improved dramatically and she concluded that this was mainly due to drinking water drawn from a well at the back of the house. The well never ran dry in the severest droughts or froze in the coldest of weathers. On analysis the water was said to contain Epsom Salts. Within a short space of time Mrs Clay had set up a 'Spa', run from her own house, and was extolling the virtues of the waters. A long list of cures were claimed for ailments such as asthma, coughs, rickets, arthritis, headaches and disorders of the blood. Mrs Clay's recommended solution was to drink one and a half pints of water at least four times a day straight from the well. So successful was Mrs Clay with her marketing that the business came to the attention of investors in London.

In 1843 a London solicitor, appropriately named Henry Fawcett of Fawcett and Co., assumed control of the business and engaged the services of well-known architect James Lockyer. This resulted in a new pump room being built further down Spa Road and the construction of the present day Spa Hotel.

The pump room was created in the form of a Grecian temple. Within this structure floor to ceiling mirrors lined the walls and impressive chandeliers hung from the ceiling. There were elegant marble fireplaces at either end of the main room. No expense was spared on the new hotel which was considered exceedingly luxurious.

Alas, the anticipated great throng of visitors never materialised. There were no bathing facilities and the clientele, as well as having the desire to take the waters, wanted day and night entertainment. Sadly Hockley could not supply what was available in the big spa towns like Bath and Harrogate.

There was more misfortune for the new owners. The spa's completion in the 1850s coincided with the opening of the London to Southend railway. Londoners, potentially the spa's biggest customers, could now get to Southend quickly to indulge in the new fad of sea bathing. For some years Hockley Spa struggled on.

A daily delivery service of bottled water to London by cart was

Hockley Spa's Pump Room

introduced. This failed however, due to unsubstantiated rumours of contamination.

In 1873 the pump room, long since closed, was leased as a Baptist chapel. Later it became a billiard room. During the 20th century it saw service as a tea-room, a shirt factory and in the manufacture of billiard tables. Much of the time it was closed and served as a store. The pump room is now a private dwelling although the exterior façade has been retained.

THE FIRST CHIEF CONSTABLE

Prior to 1840 law enforcement was hit and miss
The Essex magistrates decided, 'we can't have this,
A County wide Police Force is what's required'.
On February 11th the first Police Chief was hired.

Before 1840 the standard of policing in Essex depended largely on where one lived. Saffron Walden, Maldon, Colchester and Harwich had their own police forces each with their own chief and a staff of perhaps 20 officers, most of whom were part time. Since 1830, in the west of the county, the parts of Essex in 'East London' such as Ilford and Dagenham came under the jurisdiction of the Metropolitan Police. The remainder of Essex was left to its own devices and the law was enforced by an assortment of local watch committees, part time parish constables, the military, customs and excise and the coastguard.

Against this background Parliament passed the Constabulary Act in 1839 which authorized county councils to employ county wide paid police forces. The qualification for being a police officer was that the candidate should be between 25 and 40 years old, medically fit and over 5 feet 6 inches in height. An ability to read and write was desirable but not considered essential. Essex was one of the first to approve such a force. Neighbouring Hertfordshire and Kent, however, decided against the measure on the grounds that the paid police force in London had failed to stop crime.

The first task for Essex in setting up its own police force was to recruit a Chief Constable. On the 11th February 1840 County Magistrates convened in Shire Hall, Chelmsford to conduct interviews that took all day. There were thirty applicants for the post and nineteen were interviewed. After much deliberation Captain John Bunch Bonnemaison McHardy was selected.

McHardy, an ex-naval commander originally from the Bahamas, had won recognition for his efforts in suppressing the slave trade. Once in the post he organized his new command by strengthening its links with existing boroughs that had their own town forces as well as with the coastguard and customs and excise officers. The basic requirements to become an Essex police officer were upgraded too. Candidates, in addition to age, fitness and height and being trustworthy, were now required to read and write!

The new Chief Constable was enthusiastic about standardizing procedures and issuing written orders.

On March 13th 1840 thirteen men swore an oath before Chelmsford magistrates to become the county's first full time police officers. By June McHardy headed an Essex Police force strength of 115 (all ranks) with a police budget that year of just under £10,000. Administratively the county force was still divided into Hundreds. For example 'The Rochford Hundred', which included Southend-on-Sea, Rayleigh and Rochford, boasted one superintendent and seven constables and 'The Waltham Hundred', which included Epping, Waltham Cross and Chingford, had a superintendent, Thomas Goodwin, and four constables.

Within 20 years Saffron Walden and Harwich had amalgamated with Essex as did Maldon in 1889 and Colchester in 1947. Southend-on-Sea left in 1914, to form its own municipal police force with its own Chief Constable, only to rejoin Essex in 1969.

In the early years not everybody was happy with the new county force. Some ratepayers thought the whole enterprise was a waste of money. Soon complaints began to circulate that, in spite of all the extra expense, a policeman was never around when needed. There was also friction at times between the Police and established borough or parish constables, as well as the army, over whose jurisdiction prevailed. Nevertheless McHardy worked diligently using his considerable skills to make the county an exemplary police force. Soon favourable reports concerning 'The Boys in Blue' began to appear in the press.

When John McHardy was selected to become the first Chief Constable of Essex one of the stipulations was that the candidate should be under 45 years of age. Thus it seems quite remarkable, or perhaps a tribute to his great skills, that he remained in post for 40 years and retired a month short of his 80th birthday.

THE COGGESHALL GANG

"The 'Coggeshall Gang' as they came to be known
Were a blot on the history of that peaceable town."

The *Essex Standard* of June 1838 reported that, "for some time past the neighbourhood of Coggeshall has been infested with a gang of housebreakers, who have carried out their work in a most audacious manner". It was to be another ten years before the perpetrators of these crimes were brought to justice.

The Witham division of the Essex Constabulary, formed in 1840, had a superintendent, Charles Cooke, and two officers, with two more stationed at Coggeshall. Burglaries returned with a vengeance between 1844 and 1848 accompanied by appalling violence which brought a reign of terror to the area. Apprehending this gang was to prove a tough test for the new police force.

If the gang had a headquarters it was probably the 'Black Horse Inn' where landlord William French, half-brother to the gang's leader, Samuel Crow, was, it transpired, the fence through which the stolen goods were dispersed. The gang was made up of between ten and fourteen men, with Crow as a well-known driver of post chaises for the local gentry, well placed to identify likely targets for them.

In 1844 the unoccupied home of Charles Skinner, in Coggeshall, was burgled. Only a quantity of wine was stolen but the thieves then burned his house down. In 1845 the 'Bird in Hand' pub in East Street and the grocer, Richard Bell's, warehouse were burgled as well as many private houses. In one of these the owner was threatened with a pistol and nearly suffocated under a mattress whilst the gang drank his wine before stealing his gold and silver.

Things reached crisis level when four members of the gang broke into the house of James Finch and his housekeeper. They were both held over an open fire to make them tell where their money was kept. The housekeeper was seriously burned after her clothes caught alight. James Finch had a rope tied round his neck and nearly died when hauled up on a rafter. Ignoring their victims, the thieves ate and drank before escaping with £6 and all the provisions they could carry.

The police were getting nowhere until in 1847 a constable caught one of the gang, William Wade. He was convicted and while in Chelmsford prison awaiting transportation he had a disagreement with Samuel Crow who had reneged on a promise to look after his wife. Wade informed on the gang and arrest warrants were promptly issued.

The criminals fled or went into hiding but the police, now armed with names, were hot on their trail. Two of them, Payne and Whittaker, were arrested on board a steamer about to leave Liverpool for New York. The leader, Samuel Crow, was later arrested aboard another steamship, the *James Watt* which was bound for Hamburg. The rest of the gang were caught within Essex and brought to trial at Chelmsford Assizes in March 1849. Samuel Crow, William Tansley and William 'Crusty' Ellis were sentenced to transportation for life for their assault on James Finch. Crow died in prison before the sentence was carried out. However, his fifteen-year-old brother received three months hard labour for helping him in a bid to escape.

William Wade received fifteen years transportation, reduced to seven because he had turned queen's evidence. They were all lucky to be sentenced to transportation. Their modus operandi was very similar to that of Dick Turpin a hundred years earlier and he was sent to the gallows. Only twenty years earlier James Cook of Witham had been hanged, as an example to others, for something he didn't do.

TRIUMPH and DISASTER IN BOW CREEK

The First Lord smashed a bottle of wine over her bow.
"God speed the 'Warrior' - your time is now"

December 1860 was one of the coldest for 50 years. Bow Creek, opposite today's O2 arena, where the River Lea joins the Thames, was thick with ice. On land frozen snow covered the shipyard and icicles hung like daggers from roofs and pipes. Frost encrusted cranes sparkled as if decked in gems. Against this backdrop, the Thames Iron Works, just inside Essex, was to be the setting of not just a national first but an international one too.

It was the 29th of the month and hundreds of braziers blasted out heat as two thousand men worked to ensure the vessel would be ready on time. Crowds of spectators of all ages, including old men and young babies wrapped against the winter's chilling bite, grew by the hour. There were thousands scrambling to find a vantage point. Inside the dock the hull of the *Warrior* rose tall. Every launch from the shipyard was an event in itself but this one was going to be a celebration of national pride and triumph. Sir John Pakingham MP stepped up to perform the launch ceremony; the *Warrior* however refused to move. Despite dozens of burning braziers placed close to the hull, the iron keel would not budge. Tugs were called in to give extra leverage and shipyard workers on the upper deck ran from side to side trying to rock the vessel free. After 20 minutes, and accompanied by a great cheer, the *Warrior* finally broke away and eased down the slipway.

The launch heralded a new chapter in maritime history. At a stroke all existing warships became out of date. The *Warrior's* vital components, main guns, engines and boilers were encased inside an armoured iron hull. The revolutionary design offered power from both steam and sail. New breech loading guns and a powerful engine meant that the ship could outrun and outgun all others. At 10,000 tons it was one of the biggest ships afloat. It was remarkable that a vessel of such size could be launched in the confined area of Bow Creek. By way of comparison the *Warrior* is almost the same size as the World War II cruiser *HMS Belfast* that is permanently moored in the Thames opposite the Tower of London.

Nearly 40 years later, disaster struck the Thames Iron Works. *The Albion* was a first-class cruiser which the Admiralty had commissioned at the height of the Anglo-German naval race. The launch was due to take place in the summer of 1898 on the 21st June. Thirty thousand spectators had crammed into the shipyard to watch the Duchess of York perform the launching ceremony. Parallel to the *Albion* was a temporary slipway 'bridge'. Two hundred spectators, desperate to get a good view of the launch, had forced their way onto it despite desperate warnings from the police and yard workers that it was extremely dangerous.

As had been the case with the *Warrior*, the launch was beset with problems. Following three failed attempts to smash a bottle of champagne against the hull, which is always thought to be a sign of bad luck, the Duchess finally cut the cord and the *Albion* slid down the slipway, slowly gaining speed.

The momentum of the vessel as it hit the water created a huge wave which raced across the narrow Bow Creek and engulfed the temporary slipway bridge, smashing it to pieces, and throwing the spectators into the river. Their cries of panic were drowned out by the cheers of the main crowd applauding the launch who were completely unaware of the catastrophe, as were the Duke and Duchess of York.

It was at least ten minutes before news of the accident filtered through to the yard managers. Nearby spectators and workers begun immediate rescue efforts and some dived into the muddy waters to try and pull out survivors.

The newly formed ironworks ambulance corps was soon on the scene. Yet, despite their best efforts, 38 people, including women and children, died in the incident.

For half a century the Thames Iron Works was the most important shipyard in the country. During the 75 years of its life, until it closed in 1912, over 600 ships were built – from small cutters to great dreadnoughts. At its peak 7,000 workers were employed there. One ship, the cargo passenger-gunboat Yavari, was even crated up in kit form and sent to Lake Titicaca, two miles above sea level in Peru, where it was assembled. The *Albion* disaster was the beginning of the end for the shipyard. Ship building ceased in 1911 following the completion of the *Thunderer*, the navy's biggest warship to date. Its construction bankrupted the yard. The Thames Iron Works could not compete with the rapidly expanding shipyards of the north-east of England who had better access to coal and iron and longer slipways.

Nevertheless, the Thames Iron Works legacy lives on. West Ham United Football Club (The Hammers) had its origins in the yard's social club. Crossed Hammers like those used in ship construction appear on the club's logo.

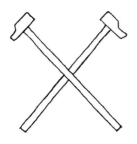

Despite all the hype at its launch the *Warrior* had an undistinguished career. Never once had it fired a shot in anger and it soon fell victim to rapidly evolving warship technology. Today the fully restored *Warrior* can be seen in Portsmouth harbour. As for the *Albion*, she saw service in the Mediterranean during World War I and was then sold for scrap in 1919.

THAMES BARGE

Out there she lies, sedately on the tide,
A legacy of dim-departed seas

Every day hundreds of heavy goods vehicles thunder along the roads of Essex taking goods into London and beyond. Comparisons between a 40-ton truck and a Thames sailing barge may seem absurd. Yet 120 years ago the sailing barges, on the waterways of Essex and into the capital, were the HGVs of the day, carrying the essentials to build, repair, fuel and feed the capital. Today there are about 30 seaworthy sailing barges left; they are used for recreation, charter work and racing. Once at least 5,000 such vessels worked in and around Essex, making a magnificent sight as they glided gently by with their tan sails framed in the rich colours of the setting sun.

The barges, with their shallow draft, were robust and relatively inexpensive to build. Their ability to take large and bulky cargoes made them cost effective. A familiar sight were the hay barges with hay stacked 12 or even 20 feet high*; one man stood on top passing instructions to the other at the tiller who could not see where he was going. It was common for just two people to sail a barge carrying 100 tons of cargo. To carry similar loads on land would have required a hundred horse-drawn carts plus one hundred drivers!

Thames Barges were a development of a craft that had been around since medieval times. The first Essex sailing barge was built in Rettendon in 1791, records would suggest, and the last in Mistley in 1928. The Thames

Barges came of age during the Napoleonic Wars, survived and even expanded through the advent of steam.

The golden age of the Thames Barge was the early to mid-1800s. This was also the great era of railway building, which eventually would be the barge's biggest competitor. Ironically it was often the barges that carried building materials to strategic points, thus speeding railway construction and, from 1860 onwards, their own gradual decline.

In the First World War, sailing barges made significant contributions to supplying the troops and in the Second World War they played a key part in the evacuation of Dunkirk. After the First World War the decline of sea-going, cargo carrying barges accelerated. New maritime safety standards were introduced that required additional crew. In some instances the owners were reluctant to fit auxiliary engines, as this would cost money to fuel them. In the end the barges could not compete with the modern alternatives, namely the articulated truck. Notwithstanding this, there were still barges carrying commercial cargoes when Neil Armstrong set foot on the moon.

*The so called stackies carried hay from the country side to London to feed the capital's horses which were used to pull the carriages and buses of the time. In many cases the return cargo was what was described as the 'London muck'. In the next chapter we encounter the Reverend Baring Gould who was not best pleased about this cargo.

ONWARD, CHRISTIAN SOLDIERS

The opening lines of the immortal hymn
Written by the Rector of East Mersea on a whim.

"It's bleak and inhospitable - the ends of the earth. I cannot say that I either liked the place or became attached to the people. The peasants were dull, shy and suspicious, I never managed to understand them. The dialect is markedly vulgar and the children of the parish uncouth. There were no resident gentry. As far I could see there were not many persons of value with whom to make friends. Then there was the London muck*- the stench was horrible – and the swarms of mosquitoes… "

Comments like this normally provoke outrage in the local community and especially more so if made by one its leading members; the Rector! Yet, over 130 years later, these comments of the Reverend Sabine Baring-Gould are affectionately quoted in local guide books for East Mersey. Baring-Gould arrived at East Mersey on March 21st 1871 as the new Rector of the Church of St Edmund. His comments cannot have endeared him to his parishioners, though his description of the island as the ends of the earth may be understandable. During his tenure there was no proper road connection to the mainland and crossing, in winter, in the dark, was a risky business. Until the end of the First World War nearly all of the island's essentials were brought in by boat as was the 'London muck' .

Baring-Gould and his wife Grace had a large family, they would eventually have fifteen children, and had outgrown the accommodation at Dalton near Thirsk, where he was rector. They moved from Yorkshire to Essex after the Prime Minister, William Gladstone, confirmed his appointment at St Edmund's.

The rector had already achieved some celebrity status with the publication of his hymn *Onward Christian Soldiers* which he said was written in ten minutes. Although he mused that the rhymes were faulty and not well based, he completely ignored changes suggested by the church hierarchy. Nevertheless, the hymn was an instant success and has become one of the best known rousing evangelistic hymns.

Baring-Gould was a prolific writer completing over 100 booklets and novels in his lifetime. One reason mooted for his leaving Yorkshire was that he needed a new challenge and the post on Mersea Island offered plenty of scope for new writing material.

On arrival in Essex, the Baring-Gould began writing one of his most compelling fictional works *Mehalah*, the tragic story of a beautiful girl 'Glory' and the violently tempered Elijah Rebow. It is based on local characters and set against a backdrop of their grim surroundings. The author spared no effort in describing the dull and desperate lives of his creations and their surroundings.

Mehalah was first published in 1880 and is still in print. Being so busy with his writing and tending to the needs of his large family, it is questionable how much pastoral care the rector could give to the parishioners of East Mersea. Whether his flock appreciated being portrayed as characters in the novel *Mehalah* is debatable too.

After 10 years in Essex, Sabine Baring-Gould moved again, this time back to his native Devon. There he continued to write and preach until his death at the age of 89 in 1924.

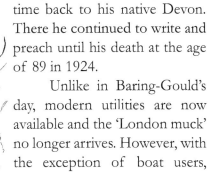
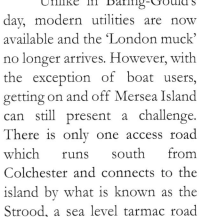

Unlike in Baring-Gould's day, modern utilities are now available and the 'London muck' no longer arrives. However, with the exception of boat users, getting on and off Mersea Island can still present a challenge. There is only one access road which runs south from Colchester and connects to the island by what is known as the Strood, a sea level tarmac road crossing. During the higher spring tides the Strood is covered by water and becomes impassable except for vehicles with high ground clearance.

* *London muck. These were the Reverend Sabine Baring-Gould's very own words. He described them it in great detail as the 'sweepings of London streets' collected in the age of horse drawn transport. The 'muck' was brought on a daily basis from the capital by Thames Barge and used as manure on the fields.*

THE SEA WITCH

She foretold the sex of the unborn child
And could say what the future would hold.
To upset her would risk a terrible curse
That might last for generations to come.

Many parts of Essex have been associated with witches and witchcraft. In 1998 the opening of 'The Sarah Moore' pub in Leigh-on-Sea commemorated the town's infamous 'Sea Witch', as Mother Moore became known in the 19th century.

In mid-Victorian times Sarah Moore lived in a tiny cottage off Victoria Wharf in what is now known as Leigh Old Town. From contemporary accounts she looked the archetype witch, weather-beaten and toothless, with a hooked nose and a harelip. If appearances were not enough she had a mean disposition and most people would try to avoid upsetting her.

Sheila Pitt-Stanley, in her book, *Legends of Leigh*, quotes personal evidence of the Sea Witch affecting her family. In 1850 her great-great grandmother, Eliza, expecting her third baby, was confronted by Sarah Moore, offering to tell the sex of the unborn child. Her brusque refusal resulted in the retort; "you're worried about having one more mouth to feed ain't yer? But mark my words, not one mouth, but two mouths....and my mouth it will be". At this Eliza slapped her face, only to be cursed that her female line would forever bring up their children alone. Pitt-Stanley confirms in her book that succeeding generation of her family through the female line this tragically happened.

There are many legends of Sarah Moore's misdeeds. On the anniversary of her son's death from cholera, in a jealous rage she cursed five babies in the town and all died within three weeks. The most legendary tale of the Sea Witch relates to her death. A skipper refused to buy a fair wind and laughed at her. Boarding his boat he was no sooner out at sea than a great squall blew up catching the boat which keeled over. One of the crew cried, "it's the witch!" The Skipper, fearing that the rigging would take them down, grabbed an axe and shouting, "I'll kill that witch!, struck the rigging three times. On the third stroke the storm ceased abruptly and the boat was able to limp home.

Approaching Leigh they were horrified to see the slumped figure of the Sea Witch, dead, from what looked like three blows of an axe.

SOUTHEND WATCH VESSEL NO 7

Watch Vessel Number Seven, no more to function.
Sold for salvage, destined for destruction.
Abandoned on the banks of the River Roach
Now lies deep in the mud of Pagelsham Reach.

Southend Watch Vessel No 7 began life as *HMS Beagle*, a Cherokee Class, 10-gun sailing ship. It was launched in Woolwich in 1820. The *Beagle*, was kept in reserve for five years, then refitted as a survey ship and made a four-year voyage to South America surveying Patagonia and Tierra Del Fuego. In 1831, Captain Robert Fitzroy invited the 22 year old Charles Darwin to be the expedition naturalist on what became known as *The Voyage of The Beagle*. This epic five year voyage is mostly remembered for Darwin's observations, which led to his theories on evolution, published as *On The Origin Of Species* in 1859. In 1845 with her days of exploration over *HMS Beagle* was transferred, to the Customs and Excise service.

Renamed *Southend Watch Vessel No 7* the vessel was used in anti-smuggling patrols along the Essex coast. An 1847 chart shows it moored in the River Roach. There it played a part in intercepting smugglers bringing in contraband along the maze of rivers, channels and creeks that criss-crossed East Coast Essex. Moved ashore to a fixed mooring in 1850, *the Beagle* became the home of customs officers and their families. The last known record of the vessel, dated 1870, is that it was sold for scrap for £525.

Its whereabouts remained a mystery until in 1997 Professor Colin Pillinger of the Open University proposed a plan for a space capsule to land on Mars. Accepted by the European Space Agency the project became known as *Beagle 2*, commemorating Darwin's voyage of discovery. Pillinger asked marine archaeologist, Dr Robert Prescott from St Andrews University, to help local researchers in searching for the original *HMS Beagle*.

In 2004, a research team led by Prescott using ground penetrating radar, and with technical help from the Mars *Beagle 2* team, located what they believe to be the remains of HMS Beagle. Her last resting place would appear to be in a sunken dock, covered in four to five meters of mud, on the banks of the River Roach close to Potton Island. The discovery suggests that the bulk of the ship is intact and in theory could be raised and restored.

COALHOUSE FORT

The big black guns were tried and tested in thin air,
But not a shot was fired in war.

For over 1,000 years castles, gun batteries and forts have been built on the Essex side of the Thames Estuary. Coalhouse Fort, located at East Tilbury, is one of them. Their purpose was to defend the country, especially the river approaches to London, from foreign invaders. However there is little to suggest that they played any useful part in defending the realm in spite of the huge cost of continually rebuilding and maintaining them.

The fortifications proved totally ineffective in June 1667 when a Dutch fleet, under the command of Admiral Michiel de Ruyter, brazenly sailed up the Thames. The Dutch fleet proceeded to threaten Tilbury but then sailed down the River Medway to sink or burn the cream of the British Navy - the *Royal James*, the *Loyal London,* and the *Royal Oak*. To add further humiliation the Dutch seized the Duke of York's flagship, the *Royal Charles*, and towed it back to Holland.

Tilbury Fort was rebuilt soon after the Dutch incursion. It was another 200 years before Coalhouse Fort was built in its present form on the site of existing gun batteries. An 1860 Royal Commission recommended building a series of coastal forts, named after the Prime Minister of the day, Lord Palmerston. Coalhouse Fort was one of them. However it was not completed for another 14 years. The finished fort had 5-foot thick walls. The roofs, made of brick and concrete, were also protected by granite and iron shields.

By the time the fort was ready the rapidly changing technology of gunnery and munitions rendered it obsolete. The casemated heavy-duty structure of Coalhouse Fort restricted the angle of firing the guns or replacing them with newer ones. Practice firings were kept to a minimum as windows could be broken in Tilbury from the shock waves. The life of a gunner was particularly miserable too, due to the deafening noise and choking black smoke in the confines of the casement. Throughout Coalhouse Fort's life guns came and went. The Fort had never fired a defensive shot in anger until the Second World War when operational (anti-aircraft) guns were placed on the roof. Since 1983 the fort has been leased to the Coalhouse Fort Project. Coalhouse is considered to be one of the finest examples of an armoured casemated fort in the United Kingdom.

THE LOPPER OF LOUGHTON

Lopping was granted by ancient right,
Not to be surrendered without a fight.

Forest and woodland once covered virtually all of Wanstead to Waltham Abbey and out to Romford. Epping Forest, today, is but a tiny fraction of the once mighty wooded area that existed in Tudor times. Yet even the forest that remains might well have disappeared but for the efforts of one man, Thomas Willingale.

Forests had been royal preserves since Norman times to a greater or lesser extent. Much of this changed because of the 'Forest Charter' of 1217, and over time the area designated as forest and therefore exclusively 'royal' diminished greatly. Yet royalty still held considerable power over what forest remained. In an act of generosity Queen Elizabeth granted a charter giving rights to householders (the commoners), who lived in the forest, to cut wood for fuel and to graze their cattle. However it was still strictly forbidden to hunt deer or other game, this was the exclusive privilege of the king or queen of the day.

Very strict rules were laid down on the practice of cutting wood, which was known as lopping. Lopping was permitted between 11th November and 23rd April (St George's Day) and could only be carried out on Mondays. Only one adult per household could lop. Wood acquired had to be removed on sledges, not wheeled carts and no more than two horses were allowed to draw the sledge. Furthermore it was forbidden to lop branches lower than seven feet from the ground. Wood obtained was to be burnt as domestic fuel and could not be sold or used for any trade purpose.

As London expanded, more and more forest was cut down for housing, industry and agriculture. In 1858 the crown sold the rights of most of Epping forest, plus 1,400 acres of land, to William Whitaker Maitland, the then Lord of the Manor at Loughton. His grandson John inherited the manor and decided to fence off parts of the forest and to ban lopping from his estate.

Thomas Willingale (a commoner) had other ideas and jealously guarded his lopping rights. Meticulously every year at midnight on 11th November, he went into the forest to begin lopping as he firmly believed that if no one started lopping at the appointed hour, the rights would be lost forever.

However, with the clandestine backing of the local board of works, Maitland decided to prosecute and for 10 years a legal game of cat and mouse went on. One year Maitland even tried to get Thomas Willingale drunk on the eve of the lopping hour in the hope of tricking him into forfeiting his lopping rights. Willingale died in 1870 but his son, Sam, took up the standard of the loppers. Over the years several fines were imposed on the Willingales. Most of these were not paid and Sam even spent some time in prison for non-payment. The case became a cause célèbre and was viewed as a David and Goliath contest. The Willingales attracted considerable moral, and then financial, support from the City of London and the House of Commons.

There was still lingering outrage at the way much of Hainault Forest had been destroyed 20 years earlier, and growing alarm at the way huge areas of Epping Forest were being fenced off for the personal gain of a few landowners whilst at the same time the public at large were denied access.

Maitland, in turn, was confronted by a series of legal challenges undertaken by the Corporation of London, which culminated in the Epping Forest Act of 1878. This declared all the enclosures made by land owners in the previous 25 years illegal and henceforth the forest was to become a public open space. The lopping rights ended too but the existing 'loppers' were financially compensated. A sum of money was also put aside to build the Lopping Hall on Loughton High Road.

The forest had been saved and unwittingly the Lopper of Loughton, Thomas Willingale, had been the saviour. Although Epping Forest lies in Essex, the City of London Corporation remains the Conservator of the Forest.

WILLIAM MORRIS

His colours reflect the landscape,
of Essex rolling downs.
Each thread or blade of grass. And stitch of golden corn.

William Morris was born in 1834, at Elm House in Walthamstow, to prosperous middle class parents. His father's rising fortunes allowed a move from this house, when William was six, to the far grander Woodford Hall. After his father's death the family moved to Water House which is today the home of the William Morris Gallery.

Morris left Walthamstow for Oxford University in 1853. Despite wealth and a privileged upbringing, he later embraced the ideas of Karl Marx and became a founding member of the Socialists. He had seen the way that the industrialisation of the nineteenth century had dehumanised production with its emphasis on the 'division of labour'. His answer to what he saw as 'the dull squalor of civilization' was to turn away from mechanisation and seek inspiration from history and nature and draw heavily on the experiences of his Essex childhood.

In the 1830s Walthamstow was little more than a village, bounded by the River Lea and its marshlands to the west, and by green fields and forest. It was an ideal setting for William's imaginative young mind to develop. Water House was impressive. It was a moated house with a spectacular black and white marble entrance leading to a massive chestnut staircase. In later life Morris was to say of Epping Forest that as a boy he knew it 'yard by yard from Wanstead to the Theydons, and from Hale End to The Fairlop Oak'. Through the forest he came to know the trees, the shapes of their leaves and the birds and wildlife that inhabited them. He was familiar with the rivers and marshes and the fish and waterbirds of the Lea and its tributaries.

Morris was fascinated by the ancient earthworks in the forest; Loughton Camp, an early iron age encampment, and Ambresbury Banks, an iron age hill-fort, both reputedly once fortified by King Arthur as a defence against encroaching Saxons.

He discovered Queen Elizabeth's Hunting Lodge at Chingford, originally built as a grandstand from which Henry VIII could watch the hunt on Chingford plain. Going inside, his imagination was fired by the faded greenery of the tapestries hanging in the medieval manner and the sheer romanticism of the place. All these experiences and scenes from his early years provided images that would be drawn on again and again in his designs.

After graduating from Oxford he became an artist but design was his real forte. A natural business man, he set up workshops to produce things by hand, with the emphasis on creating beauty while blending usefulness with truth to material and sound design. His products were an immediate success. His designs of wallpapers, fabrics, furniture and interior decoration made a worldwide impact which is still being felt today.

It was a number of young men in the 1880s, developing their interest in traditional hand crafts and inspired by Morris, who gradually came together to form what became, 'The Arts and Crafts Movement'. William Morris is often associated with the Arts and Crafts Movement; he was not its founder though he was certainly its inspiration.

The William Morris Gallery, was opened Saturday 21st October 1950 by Prime Minister Clement Attlee and is the only public museum devoted to Morris and his works. The Gallery is set in its own grounds, which now form Lloyd Park.

William Morris is probably best remembered today for his designs of patterned wallpapers and woven fabrics. Examples of these, imitating the flow of water, shapes of birds, the curl of their feathers, the different leaves and their spring and autumn colourings are on display. Some of them are no doubt drawn from recollections of his idyllic Essex childhood.

EARTHQUAKE

In less than a minute some twelve hundred buildings
Were damaged or shattered by waves in the round.
Churches lost battlements. Towers and spires,
Broken and rent, tumbled down to the ground.

On the morning of Tuesday 22nd April 1884 at 9.18am precisely, Essex was struck by one of the strongest earthquakes ever to hit the British mainland. It was estimated to have measured 5.1 on the Richter scale. The epicentre was between Colchester and Wivenhoe. The quake lasted for about 20 seconds. By the time it was over an enormous amount of property damage had been wrought in the county. The financial cost was huge and as usual the burden fell more heavily on the less well off as poor housing suffered terribly in the destruction.

An eyewitness, Mr. William Ham, gave a dramatic account of the events in Wivenhoe which was later printed in the *Essex Telegraph*. At the time of the earthquake Mr. Ham was working on a boat moored on the River Colne facing the village. He was quoted as saying 'the first indication I had that anything was amiss was that the vessel rose a foot'. He went on to report that, as the earthquake shock rolled through the village, every single chimney toppled producing clouds of dust and soot that completely obscured the view.

Although the earthquake lasted only a few seconds, whole villages were wrecked and Colchester was reduced to a state of panic and chaos. In 1884 there was no electric lighting, no telephones, no radio or television and the great majority of people had no idea what an earthquake was. All over the area tiles and chimneys crashed to the ground as roofs collapsed, glass shattered, walls bent and church steeples cracked. The shock was felt as far away as Cheshire and the Isle of Wight although no damage was reported there. Fortunately there were no deaths directly attributable to the earthquake, contrary to some local stories filed at the time. The fact that the earthquake happened in daylight, unlike more recent tremors in this country, may have been a life saver too.

There were a number of lucky escapes which included a fisherman on Southend pier who was tossed into the water by the shock and then plucked from the sea by quick thinking colleagues.

There was no shortage of enterprise willing to profit from the disaster. Bearing in mind photography was in its infancy, it is quite remarkable that within days sets of photographs of damaged buildings were being advertised for sale in newspapers. The Great Eastern Railway Company got in on the act too and put on extra trains to bring sightseers to the devastated areas. By the following weekend 2,000 visitors were arriving in Colchester on a daily basis by train alone.

Suddenly all sorts of building tradesmen appeared on the scene making extravagant claims about their craftsmanship and honesty. One Colchester man even suggested that a few damaged buildings should be left untouched as a reminder of the earthquake and as a potential tourist attraction!

On a brighter note, a disaster fund was established almost immediately and by the end of July most of the damage inflicted had been repaired. As an odd coincidence, 1884 was a leap year as were the dates of three of the five other recent quakes to strike in this country.

Panic and Confusion following the Earthquake

TIPTREE JAM

'By their fruits shall ye know them'
Strawberries, raspberries, gooseberries and cherries,
Glorious fruit all there for the picking
At Tiptree - the land of superior jams.

Tiptree Jam has a reputation that has spread beyond Essex, England and Europe to places as far flung as America, Australia, Israel and Hong Kong. The village of Tiptree in Essex and the Wilkin family inextricably are linked. In 1885, the Wilkins' had already been farming fruit in Tiptree for two hundred years. The fruit was taken to market by horse and cart.

Increasingly concerned over damage to the fruit in transit, Arthur Wilkin began making his own preserves. The experiment was so successful that he formed a company under the name 'Britannia'. The venture flourished and before long he decided to use his own name, changing the company to 'Wilkin and Sons Ltd'. Arthur was also the prime mover in establishing the privately owned Kelvedon, Tiptree and Tollesbury light railway line. The line opened in 1904 and was affectionately called the 'Crab and Winkle'. Within five years it was carrying 1,000 passengers a day plus the finished produce from Wilkin's factory. Unfortunately two World Wars, coupled with the rise of the motor vehicle, saw the railway's rapid decline. Taken over by British Rail, the line was closed in 1962.

Arthur Wilkin's company still thrives in Tiptree today with nearly half of all its production being exported. In the UK Tiptree Jams are a familiar sight in leading department stores and quality food outlets. The demand from London hotels is such that daily deliveries are made to the capital.

The success of this family run firm is the result of generations of Wilkins sticking to the basic philosophy of their founder. The firm has relied upon the people of Tiptree since its beginning. In return it has recognised their contribution and treated them well. Many staff take more than just an employee interest in the business and family involvement is strong.

Some fifty years ago John Wilkin began collecting the paraphernalia of jam making, preserving and Essex Life. The items he brought together now form the basis of the Tiptree Museum which was opened in October 1995 along with a tearoom.

GIVE US BACK OUR ESSEX

Bishops Stortford's Poor Law Union Board
Had villages in Essex and Herts to care for.
Paying the least they were forced to afford
Barely keeping the poorest from death's door.

Stansted Hall has had many illustrious owners. At the time of the Doomsday Book Robert Gernon owned the estate. It then passed to the Montfichets who gave their name to Stansted Mountfitchet. It was part of the de Vere family estate in the fifteenth and sixteenth centuries, apart from twenty years or so when the 12th Earl was executed by Richard III after the battle of Townton. Richard confiscated the estate, only for it to be restored to the family by Henry VII. Since then the incumbents have included Lords Mayor of London and a succession of Members of Parliament until, in the early nineteenth century, it came into the ownership of the Fuller Maitland Family.

In 1876 William Fuller-Maitland virtually rebuilt the hall, creating a mansion suitable to house his priceless art collection. This however was not, as far as Essex is concerned, his greatest achievement. In 1888 William Fuller-Maitland led a rebellion of Essex villagers against a bureaucratic proposal to change the county boundary to take five Essex villages into Hertfordshire. The Poor Law Act 1834 had led to the creation of institutions such as the Bishops Stortford Union, which took care of the poor over a wide area. Ever conscious of the need to reduce costs, the board of guardians sought to expand their scope to take in the Essex villages. In collusion with this suggestion the boundary commissioners, bureaucrats to the core who loved straight lines on maps, saw an excuse to straighten out a kink in the boundary line. This would mean that Elsenham, Farnham, Manewdon, Stansted and Ugley would become Hertfordshire villages.

The plan met with fierce opposition and cries of, "We have been Essex Men since Alfred the Great". This opposition was organised into a co-ordinated protest by Joseph Green, a storekeeper, backed up by the considerable political weight of Fuller-Maitland. Under this storm of well organised opposition the authorities were obliged to back down and the plan was abandoned.

KYNOCHTOWN

Kynochtown was renamed as old patrons had gone,
And the new village in the oil refinery was called Coryton.

The peninsular on which the new village of Kynochtown was founded in 1897 was called Shell Haven. There was no connection with the multinational oil giant of today. Shell Haven was so called after the shell bar in one of the creeks by Canvey Island.

Kynoch and Company Ltd, a Birmingham based munitions manufacturer, was looking to expand and chose a site on the marshes to build an explosives factory. The second Boer war in South Africa was looming and the extra capacity would help to cope with the expected upsurge in demand for munitions. Coincidentally the Chairman of Kynoch was a brother of the then Colonial Secretary Joseph Chamberlain.

To accommodate the workforce a village was built which originally consisted of forty houses, a school and a shop that also served as a post office. The official naming of Kynochtown took place in 1899. By 1903 a working mans' club called 'The Institute' had been added. The company also bought land on Canvey Island on which they built the Kynoch Hotel. Hotel guests visiting the factory were rowed across Shell Haven creek. During the Second World War the Kynoch Hotel accommodated military personnel, it was demolished in 1960.

Although there was a constant danger from air raids during the First World War the manufacture of explosives continued until 1919. It ceased then, ostensibly due to the risk of flooding, but possibly, with the war over, a downturn in demand was the key factor. Although the factory closed but the village of Kynochtown remained.

Four years later the site was purchased by the Cardiff based Cory Brothers who proposed to construct an oil refinery and associated storage facilities. The village was also renamed Coryton. The refinery was built and over the next decade it expanded so much that the village of Coryton became completely enclosed within the complex. During the Second World War oil refining stopped and the village was used to house the military. After the war the Vacuum Oil Company (soon to be Mobil Oil) bought out Cory Brothers and began the construction of another oil refinery. In the meantime civilians had returned to the village. The new refinery came on stream in January 1953 but was then closed almost immediately by the great flood of that year. During the 1960s, as the industrial site grew, concerns were raised at the wisdom of having housing in the middle of such a potentially dangerous complex.

In the interests of safety all the villagers were gradually re-housed in Corringham and by 1974 the village had been demolished and the name Kynochtown almost completely forgotten.

Visitors transferring to the
Kynocktown Hotel on Canvey Island

LONGER THAN A MILE

Oh Southend Pier longer than a mile!
Treading your boards, walking in style.

Since 1890, when Southend's modern pier was opened, countless thousands have trod its boards. It was in the early nineteenth century that the need for a pier first surfaced. Championed by Alderman William Heygate, a former Lord Mayor of London, the first wooden pier opened in 1830. Initially 600 feet in length, it was unusable at low tide and by 1846 had been extended to 7,000 feet making it the longest pier in Europe. It was bought by the local board, later the council, in 1873.

In the last half of the 19th century the town was changing from being a quiet Essex resort. The London, Tilbury and Southend Railway brought so many visitors from London's East End that they generated the nickname of 'Whitechapel by the Sea'. In an atmosphere of growth and increasing popularity the council decided that the wooden pier should be replaced. James Brunlees designed a new iron structure complete with an all-electric railway and the new pier, which extended as far as the 'Old Pier Head', opened on 24th August 1890.

Steamships increasingly used the pier and by 1908 a 'New Pier Head' complete with upper deck, had been added. Then in 1929, the Prince George Extension brought the pier's length up to 1.34 miles; the longest pleasure pier in the world.

Half a million people enjoyed the pier in 1910. Its popularity increased year on year and despite being closed during World War Two, it reached its peak in 1949 with seven million visitors recorded. Although numbers have since decreased, they still average around half a million visitors annually.

The Pier has suffered more than its fair share of disasters. In 1959 the 'Pier Pavilion' was burned down. In its place a ten-pin bowling alley was built, opening in 1962. Then in 1976 another major fire devastated the 'New Pier Head'. Despite this, and the closure of the train service due to track damage, the pier remained open.

Ten years later in the summer of '86, the MV Kings Abbey sliced through the pier between the Old and New Pier Heads causing immense damage. This was not the first time for such an accident. William Bradley, the first pier light-keeper, and his family had lived in a bungalow on the Old Pier Head. In 1889 they were marooned when a vessel crashed through the pier in a similar fashion. They were rehoused ashore and William, who was influential in the formation of the RNLI in Southend, later became an Alderman of the Borough.

In 1995 disaster struck again when the bowling alley was completely destroyed by fire as was 30 meters of track. Nevertheless the pier was reopened within three weeks. The most recent calamity to befall the pier was in October 2005. Again it was fire that laid waste to the South Station and the Old Pier Head.

The first mile of the pier was reopened to the public on 1st December the same year and the pier head in the following August via a permanent walkway over the damaged area.

Despite all these disasters, plus the ravages of two world wars* and being requisitioned by the Navy as *HMS Leigh*, the pier has received substantial investment over the last few years.

The Royal Pavilion, a cultural centre and a café was opened in July 2012 on the pier head. Hosting theatrical, musical events and even weddings, it has confirmed the pier's status as both an asset to the town and a major visitor attraction.

On March 21st 1941 a military order was signed authorising the blowing up of Southend Pier in the event of enemy invasion.

SALVATION ARMY COLONY

The Salvation Army bought the land
High above the Old Leigh strand.
The unemployed from London towns
Were brought by Booth to Hadleigh Downs.

In his 1890 book *In Darkest England and the Way Out* General William Booth outlined proposals to help the thousands of destitute unemployed of London. The scheme was mocked and greeted with derision by many in his peer group and Booth anticipated questions from them such as: "Do you think you can create agricultural pioneers out of the scum of Cockneydom?"

To turn his plan into reality, Booth purchased 800 acres of land overlooking the Thames estuary at Hadleigh, Essex in March 1891, stipulating it should be as far away from pubs as possible. Known locally as 'the badlands', because of its poor farming quality, it became the foundation of the 'Salvation Army Farm Colony'. Eventually the estate comprised 3,200 acres and encompassed the 14th century castle, farms to the south of Hadleigh Village, Two Tree Island and stretched to the cockle sheds in Leigh. To the north the colony took in much of what is now the Highlands estate and Belfairs Park.

Hadleigh residents did not welcome the plan and were fearful of increased criminal activity. Booth however was determined. Even though a local newspaper accused him of riding roughshod over local feeling and acting as 'Baron of Hadleigh,' local antipathy was gradually overcome. The Salvation Army began to transform the neglected farms. Material was shipped by Thames Barge from the Army's City Colony at Battersea and delivered to a newly constructed dock at Hadleigh Ray. Within three months of purchase nearly 250 'Colonists' were on site busily working under the supervision of Major Wright, the Colony's first Governor.

The wide range of farming skills that were taught included care of livestock and poultry, arable farming, orchard and market gardening. A pottery and a brick making works followed and at the peak of operations three separate factories could produce 10 million bricks annually. The colonists even built their own railway line which linked the brick works to the dock and an industrial tramway to Leigh-on-Sea mainline rail station.

By the time of its 21st anniversary in 1912 the Army had trained some 7,000 colonists in skills that could give them a new start. The Colony Farm, as it came to be known, attracted some famous visitors including Cecil Rhodes and J. Rider Haggard who both praised its success.

The two World Wars and the intervening years brought great change. Wounded servicemen were accommodated during the First World War and the military requisitioned much of the land during the Second. Between the wars many colonists emigrated to new lives in Australia, South Africa and Canada, often embarking on ships sailing from Tilbury.

With the introduction of the Welfare State, following the end of the Second World War, the Colony's original aims were no longer relevant although boys on probation and young ex-offenders were still trained there. The last brick works closed in 1956 and for a brief period motorcycle scrambling events took place on the downs.

By the 1960s the farm was being run commercially, with profits going to general Salvation Army funds. Then in 1990 a new training centre was launched. Its facilities include a Tea Room, Rare Breeds Centre, the Home Farm Nursery and workshops. These provide training opportunities, in partnership with local Social Services departments, for people with learning disabilities. Over a century has passed since the inception of the colony. Much of the surrounding area to the south has been incorporated in the Country Park run by Essex County Council. In 2012 Hadleigh Farm hosted the Olympic Mountain Biking event and as part of the legacy the track has since been converted to cycling sporting hub.

THE GILBEY ACCOLADE

*"Sir, in reply to your request, the prettiest village
in the east, I would say Finchingfield
Having considered this in depth, it is so".*

As the 19th century came to an end a new leisure pursuit grew up –
cycling. Every weekend country lanes became crowded with an ever-
growing army of enthusiasts devoted to this new pursuit.

A new newspaper was also born, *The Rambler*. First published in
1897, it described itself as 'a penny newspaper devoted to outdoor life'.
The Rambler ran a feature which encouraged cyclists to explore the
countryside and nominate 'the prettiest village in England'. Over eight
weeks, the great and the good and the celebrities of the day were invited
to write to the newspaper offering their opinion.

Among those to reply was one Sir Walter Gilbey of Elsenham, near
Stansted*. In a terse letter of four lines he wrote: "In reply to your letter,
if you asked me the finest city in the United Kingdom I should say
Edinburgh; and if you asked me the prettiest village in the eastern counties
I would say Finchingfield, but beyond this I cannot go".

Gilbey was the President of the Royal Agricultural Society. His
words, published in *The Rambler* on 12th February 1898 and then picked up
by the *Essex County Chronicle*, took on a life of their own and became
known as 'The Gilbey Accolade'. They were eagerly copied by numerous
other publications and travel guides. In the decades to follow almost
nothing was printed about Finchingfield without reference to the tag line,
in spite of the varying fortunes of the village and the newspaper. *The
Rambler* went out of business within two years due in part to its small
circulation.

At the time of the 'Accolade' Finchingfield was actually in decline.
It had lost nearly a third of its population, incidents of polluted water and
bad sanitation were reported and a number of houses were considered
unfit for habitation and condemned. Nevertheless many painters were
inspired by the village and an artist's colony formed that included Lucien
Pissarro and equestrian painter Alfred Munnings. Today Finchingfield has
the reputation as the most photographed village in England.

** The return distance from Elsenham to Finchingfield is just over 40 miles
(64 km), perhaps quite an achievement for 67 year old Sir Walter on a Victorian
'boneshaker' to cover in one day.*

FAMILY COURTAULD

George Courtauld - descendant of a French refugee
Opened a silk mill in the town of Braintree.
After nine good years he retired knowing well
That the mill would be safe with son Samuel.

George Courtauld, the great grandson of a French Huguenot refugee, opened his own silk mill in Braintree in 1809. This was the beginning of a long association between Braintree and the Courtauld family. George brought his radical unitarian principles into the business and it flourished. One of the difficulties he faced as business improved was recruiting labour. Ideally silk spinning required young nimble fingers, preferably girls aged 10 to 13. Having exhausted the supply of young children locally, Courtauld started taking girls from 'well run' workhouses in London. The workhouse contracted to pay him £5 for each child taken and a further £5 after the first year. He insisted that each child came with 'a complete change of common clothing' and was to be a bound apprentice until the age of 21. In return he promised that his mill would 'prove a nursery of respectable young women fitted for any of the humbler walks of life'.

George Courtauld was a believer in social reform. In 1813 some of his apprentice girls ran away, claiming that their supervisor had badly beaten them. Courtauld, while disclaiming any liability, immediately dismissed the supervisor and set his four daughters the task of caring for the apprentices. They arranged a system of marks to monitor the work and behaviour of the girls. Taking their responsibilities seriously, they were setting the tone for the future, in terms of the whole family being involved in the company. The firm was regarded locally as a good employer.

In 1818 George decided to retire to live in America where he died in 1823. His son Samuel took over the mill. Under Samuel the mill thrived and he expanded with additional mills at Halstead and Bocking. An innovator, he introduced steam power to the Bocking mill and by 1835 Halstead boasted over two hundred power looms. By the mid-century the Courtauld mills employed over two thousand people.

Although it was Samuel that put the company on the road to success, it was still very much a family concern. Brothers, sisters, sons, daughters, and cousins all played their part. Samuel's wife Ellen employed a nurse and organised a crèche for working mothers, probably the first company in the country to do so. Mothers would drop their children off at 6a.m. and pick them up at 6p.m. and they would be given 'boiled rice and treacle for their dinner'. For the employees a Workmen's Institute and evening classes were set up. The firm started to become a world-wide organisation when, in 1904, Samuel's son, also Samuel, acquired the rights to the 'Viscose system'. This led to the discovery of 'Rayon' and many other 'man-made' materials which revolutionised the clothing industry as well as other products as diverse as tyres, power transmission belts, furnishing fabrics and even cigarette filters.

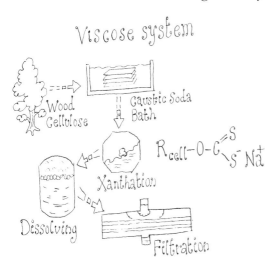

If the family were rich they were also generous and evidence of this may still be seen in Braintree. As early as 1862 George (the second) Courtauld bought the land and built Manor Street School, currently the Braintree District Museum. Then in 1871 his wife founded the Cottage Hospital in Broad Road which is now a private house. They also funded the Braintree and Bocking Institute to foster study and learning. The Public Gardens are today much as they were in 1888 when Sydney and Sarah Courtauld gave them to the town. The celebrations at this event were said to rival those for the Queen's Jubilee the previous year. Sydney's son, William Julien, continued the tradition by giving the town the William Julien Courtauld Hospital, the Fountain in the Town Square and the Town Hall.

Courtaulds was a household name in textile manufacture until the late 1980s but it succumbed to fierce competition from manufacturers in Asia. Outside Braintree, the philanthropy of the Courtaulds is still evident at *The Courtauld Institute* in London. Founded by Samuel Courtauld (IV), the company chairman until 1946, he was responsible for founding the institute whose original aims were to provide a forum for an academic study of art history.

JOSCELYNE'S BEACH CHALKWELL

"Nine Pound". She cried "Nine Pound!
To lease a stretch of shingle!"

We may all do something risky once in our lives when dealing with the family finances but Arthur Joscelyne senior's little business venture in 1909 may take some beating. One Saturday in March he rushed home from the Smack Inn in Old Leigh. A little the worse for wear, demanding lunch be put on hold, he went straight to the mantelpiece and scooped the contents out of the china jug which held all the family savings. His wife was dumfounded and asked what was going on, to which he replied, "Sorry love can't stop, I've just seen a man in a pub and I'm going to buy a beach", and without further ado he was gone.

Later that day, Ellen Elizabeth, his wife, discovered what had become of the nine pounds of savings. She was not too pleased to put it mildly. Arthur Joscelyne had purchased from the Southend and Tilbury Railway Company, a four-month, June – September, lease on a beach at Chalkwell. It was triangular in shape and measured just 200 yards in length and, when the tide was in, about 50 yards depth at its widest point.

The Chalkwell of 1909 had no station or bridge to the seafront. The railway line that ran from Leigh to Southend-on-Sea completely cut off access to the sea. On the sea side of the line a rough cinder path ran from Leigh Old Town, parallel to the track, atop crude stone sea defences. The building of the sea defences had been somewhat haphazard and as a consequence large chunks of rock littered the beach, which were a hazard to bathers and boats alike.

In spite of all the obstacles, both financial and physical, by the end of the first season Arthur Joscelyne had installed a large shed on the beach. This served as a focal point and the creation of a fine business was in the making. Ellen had now accepted the situation and wholeheartedly endorsed the project. The next year the lease was renewed. Gradually the beach was cleared of stones and rocks.

Changing tents were put up and a small fleet of boats were made available for hire and trips. Fishing was popular and the sale of bait and rods was lucrative. The business grew and even flourished during the First World War. A severe blow came in 1917 when Arthur senior died suddenly of a strangulated hernia. Ellen took the helm and Arthur junior, at the age of 14, stepped into his father's shoes. Every year throughout the 20s and

30s, including the general strike and the years of economic depression, Joscelyne's Beach was open for the summer.

However it was gradually becoming more and more difficult to maintain its privacy as Westcliff-on-Sea and Southend became established as seaside resorts. Apart from that, and the odd storm or exceptional tide that swept away the changing tents and boats, business continued as normal until the Second World War.

At the outbreak of war all the Essex beaches were closed. When the war ended Ellen, now aged seventy, resumed the business but it was short lived. In 1948 the government nationalised the railways and thus ended the leasing arrangement. Private beaches were also considered out of character in the post war Britain. Ellen died shortly afterwards. The area is still known to locals as Joscelyne's Beach and the path that runs from Leigh to Chalkwell station is still known as the cinder path, although the cinders have long since gone along with the steam trains that created them.

THAXTED

In twelve-eighty-seven one Richard de Taxte
Was known as a hafter in the village of Thaxted.

After the Norman invasion of 1066 the Saxon settlement of Thaxted became one of the 'spoils of war'. As such the Manor of Thaxted was granted by William the Conqueror to one of his supporters and relatives, Gilbert, Earl of Clare. Unlike his kinsmen de Vere, Montfitchet or de Mandeville, Gilbert did not build himself a great castle, just a grand manor house, but that disappeared during the fourteenth century.

For a time Thaxted was the home of a thriving cutlery industry and the Cutlery Guild rose to prominence. One the guild's leading members was Richard de Taxte, a hafter or maker of handles. The still functioning Thaxted Guildhall, built around 1400, is a legacy to the Cutlers Guild. The cutlery industry disappeared in the sixteenth century and the guildhall became an administrative centre for the town.

The other most significant building that has survived is the Church of St John the Baptist, St Mary and St Lawrence. Begun in about 1340, in the reign of Edward III, and completed 170 years later in the reign of Henry VIII, its 181 feet tall spire dominates the town today.

Conrad Le Dispenser Noel, the Vicar of Thaxted in the early 1900s, was appointed by the eccentric and radical socialist Countess of Warwick. Known as Daisy Greville, and once a mistress of Edward VII, she was the granddaughter of Lord Maynard of nearby Easton Lodge, one of the grandest of Essex estates, which she inherited. The Countess wholeheartedly embraced socialism and seemed to have the ambition to create a hothouse of socialist thought in and around Easton Lodge.

Conrad Noel was a man of immense charm and energy and he was loved by everyone who knew him, but his politics were, at the time, somewhat bewildering. Like the countess he was quite a radical and became known as the Red Vicar because of his left leaning sympathies. He authorised the display of the Sinn Fein Republican Flag and the Communist Red Flag, by the church altar. Although he allowed the English St George's flag to be hung he did not allow the Union Flag as he believed it to be imperialist and oppressive. He also set up a 'Chapel of John Ball, the priest and martyr of the 1381 Peasants Revolt' and hoisted a red flag on every May Day. Noel's actions caused dissent. What became known as 'The Battle of the Flags' ensued when groups of 'Empire Loyalists', students from Cambridge University, descended upon Thaxted, on May Day and prominently displayed the Union flag. They would also attempt to forcibly remove any flags not to their liking. On Empire Day, May 24th 1921, a large group laid siege to Thaxted church, to try and force the removal of the Irish Republican and Communist Flags.

Apart from politics Noel became famous for his plainsong, incense, flower-processions and folk-dancing. In 1911 Conrad Noel and his wife, Miriam, encouraged the formation of a 'Morris' club. Thus began the internationally famous tradition of the Thaxted Morris, making the town a national centre for Morris dancing. In 1934, after a meeting in Thaxted, 'The Morris Ring' was formed and for many years clubs from all over England gathered in front of the Guildhall soon after Whitsun.

The Church, built on a cathedral plan, has often been referred to as 'The Cathedral of Essex'. Its interior is no less impressive and has fine acoustic qualities. It was these that Gustav Holst, the composer, appreciated when he visited in 1913. A year later Holst came to live in a thatched cottage in Monk Street where he wrote his 'Planets' suite. In 1916 he organised the first Whitsuntide Festival in Thaxted.

The musical tradition continues to this day. In 1980 Michael Snow began the Thaxted Festival. This festival, for a number of weeks each summer, provides a series of musical events of outstanding quality in a setting visually and acoustically quite unique, in what is probably one of the finest parish churches anywhere.

I MAY BE SOME TIME.

"I'm just going outside and may be some time."
Simple words, profoundly spoken to chime

Visitors entering the village of Gestingthorpe in north Essex may puzzle over the face on the village sign. It is that of Captain Laurence Oates, who crawled out of his tent and into a blizzard with the famous parting words, "I am just going outside and may be some time". This action, in temperatures of minus 40 degrees, taken to maybe give his colleagues a better chance of survival, is the stuff of legend.

Laurence Edward Grace Oates was born on March 17th 1880 to William and Caroline Oates. In June 1891, when Laurence was eleven, the family moved into Gestingthorpe Hall. Surrounding the house was a vast park. It was here that Laurence's passion for horses began which continued after he left school when he joined the Inniskillen Dragoon Guards, a Cavalry Regiment.

As a Second Lieutenant, Oates served in the Boer War where he was shot, the bullet smashing his thighbone. In great pain and under fire he resisted repeated calls to surrender and was eventually rescued. For his bravery he was awarded the Victoria Cross. Left with a pronounced limp, he returned to Gestingthorpe to recuperate. On hearing of a planned 1,800 mile expedition to the South Pole, Oates bought himself out of the army. The expedition leader, Captain Robert Falcon Scott, planned to use Siberian ponies to haul the expedition sledges. Oates joined the team primarily as the expert on horses. Oates frequently clashed with Scott. He felt isolated as the only army man on what was essentially a naval expedition. He described the horses (bought without his knowledge) as "the greatest lot of crocks I have ever seen". During the first four hundred miles of the expedition many animals died. Those unable to work were shot and left in the frozen waste. The men now had the backbreaking task of hauling the heavy sledges. On reaching the pole they found the Norwegian, Amundsen, using dogs, had beaten them.

On the return journey Oates, starving, suffering from severe frostbite and gangrene in his feet, realised he had become a burden and was holding the others back. On the day Oates died, his leader, Scott, sensing that the end was nigh, wrote in a farewell letter "...we have been to the Pole and we shall die like gentlemen". They struggled on but all were to perish some eleven miles from the food depot that could have meant their salvation.

ESSEX FARM

The Essex Regiment saw the war through
They did their duty simply knowing what to do

Essex Farm is a First World War cemetery lying alongside the Yser canal approximately two miles north of Ypres (Ieper) in Belgium. Located in what was known as the Ypres Salient, the area was witness to some of the fiercest fighting and worst carnage of the war. It also saw the first chemical attack in the history of war when chlorine gas was used on April 22nd, 1915. Between 1914 and 1918 hundreds of thousands of British and Empire troops were based in the area

Essex Farm is just one of 160 World War I cemeteries in the area and is relatively small with 1,204 burials recorded. In contrast the Menin Gate Memorial, at the eastern exit of Ypres, has over 50,000 names of soldiers whose bodies were never found. Although Essex Farm is relatively small, there are more British soldiers buried there than those that died in service during the more recent Falklands, Iraq and Afghan wars combined.

The Essex Farm cemetery had its beginnings in early 1915 when responsibility for this area of unnamed farmland, occupied by the French Army, was transferred to the British Army. The Canadian field artillery established a small, basic dressing station on the eastern side of the canal to tend to the wounded. As the war progressed, this facility grew in size to become a more sophisticated, 'Advanced Dressing Station' or ADS. Here the injured would be examined, treated and if deemed appropriate, operated on. As the casualties mounted many of those brought in didn't survive. Thus the dressing station became home to a cemetery.

Although an engraving on the memorial at the cemetery entrance attributes the name of Essex Farm to the Essex Regiment there is no obvious reason for this. It is known that the 2nd Essex Battalion and the Essex Yeomanry were in Ypres during the spring of 1915, but so too were many other regiments. The first fatality from the Essex Regiment to be buried at Essex Farm was Private Arthur Lawrence Badkin of the 2nd Essex Battalion. Aged 27, Private Badkin, from Walthamstow, was killed in action on 9th June 1915. The Battalion's War Diary on that date records, "a quiet day with just one soldier killed". At the beginning of October 1915 the 11th Battalion of the Essex Regiment arrived in Ypres. They were deployed in the vicinity of the Yser canal bank, to the north of the town, and spent much of their time digging, repairing or manning trenches. The battalion remained in the Ypres salient until July 1916. During that time 27 of its members were killed in action and buried at Essex Farm. A significant entry in the Battalion War Diary of 13th June 1916 is that of Captain H. W. H. Creasy, the commander of C. Company. The Captain was, "killed when examining a fallen mortar bomb that suddenly blew up". The diary goes on to say, "He was buried that night at Essex Farm". This is the only reference in Essex Regimental records that relates to a burial at Essex Farm and indicates that the name Essex Farm had been adopted sometime earlier. It would seem likely that the name was adopted during the time of the 2nd Battalion, possibly at the time of Private Badkin's internment.

Essex Farm is more well-known, both nationally and internationally, from being the setting for the memorial to John McCrae, the author of one of the world's best known poems of the First World War, *In Flanders Fields*. McCrae was a surgeon in the First Brigade of Canadian Field Artillery. The poem was written following the death of his friend, Alexis Helmer, killed in action on May 2nd, whose burial service McCrae himself conducted. Later that day McCrae composed the poem sitting in the back of an ambulance. In *Flanders Fields* was later published in the magazine *Punch* in December 1915.

ZEPPELIN

Having dropped bombs on London without inhibition
The Zeppelin turned for home to complete its mission

September 1916: London was under threat from the latest German 'Super Airships'. Zeppelins (named after the German Count Ferdinand von Zeppelin) were an awesome sight. The 680 feet long, cigar shaped balloons contained two million cubic feet of gas. Their aluminium frame structure, covered by a varnish impregnated skin and weighing fifty tons, could carry a load of sixty bombs.

On the night of the 23rd of September, two Zeppelins designated L32 and L33, bombed London causing much death and destruction.

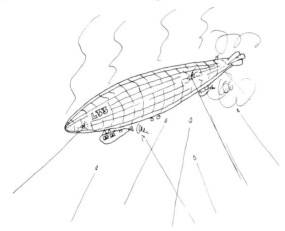

After the raid, L33 was hit by anti-aircraft fire and damaged by night fighter aircraft based at Hainault. Having just managed to limp across the Essex coast, L33's Captain Alois Böcker, on his first mission, despite jettisoning guns* and equipment into the sea, realised that he would not make it home. He turned his ship back towards Mersea. The Zeppelin eventually made a forced landing near New Hall Farm in Little Wigborough in the small hours of the morning.

Böcker's priority was to destroy the airship. Before setting fire to it, the captain knocked on the doors of nearby New Hall Cottages to warn the residents. The terrified the occupants did not open their doors. With the airship burning fiercely the Germans left and marched off in the direction of Colchester.

Special Constable Nicholas, who was cycling to investigate the blaze, met the group on the road. He dismounted and noted that their leader, although speaking good English, had a distinct 'foreign' accent. Nicholas accompanied the Germans to Peldon Post Office where they were formally identified as the enemy and arrested by PC 354 Charles Smith. Peldon did not have a Police Station and the Post Mistress declared, "They can't stay here". According to contemporary local press reports, the captured airmen were kept at a nearby church hall. PC Smith telephoned the military base at Mersea. The following day a military detachment arrived to take the Germans into army detention, thus ending the war for Böcker and his crew.

L33 was one of twelve Zeppelin airships in the skies that night. Another one, L32, after dropping its bombs on Purfleet was shot down over Burstead, near Billericay. There were no survivors from the crew of 22. For the local press it was a dramatic story. The *Essex Times* later that week ran the following headline.

TWO ZEPPELINS MEET THEIR DOOM
A WONDERFUL MIDNIGHT SPECTACLE

Today both incidents are well documented, but in 1916 the newspapers did not identify where the Zeppelins came to ground. The *Times* described L32's Burstead crash site simply as 'being on a farm'. L33's crash site was referred to as 'the other place near two timber built cottages bordering a roadway'. The *Southend Standard* produced a souvenir supplement that included numerous eyewitness reports. Their reporter, writing under the name of 'Idler', said that L33 had come down 'in a quiet creek like parish somewhere in Essex, by the coast'.

Another Essex paper, *The Barking, East Ham and Ilford Advertiser*, claimed to be the first newspaper to have had a correspondent on the scene of the crash at Burstead. Their reporter, allegedly, arrived at 3.00am only to find a large crowd already gathered with the fire brigade and the police in attendance, the latter to deter souvenir hunters.

The Essex Chief Constable, on hearing the news of PC Smith's prompt and decisive action, promoted him to the rank of Sergeant. Until he died, at the age of 94, he was known by all as 'Zepp' Smith. At nearby Great Wigborough, Mrs Clarke, of Abbotts Hall, gave birth to a daughter at about the same time as the Zeppelin was burning. The doctor attending her, Doctor Stanley, recorded in his diary that he had suggested that the baby might be christened, 'Zeppelina'. He did not record whether his advice was taken.

In a sad sequel, 45 year old Alfred Wright went out on his motorcycle to look for the fallen Zeppelin L33. On his way he collided with a car driven by George Tiffin going in the opposite direction, who was also looking for the crash site. Mr Wright suffered a compound fracture of the leg, which later had to be amputated. Unfortunately gangrene set in and he died on 13th November.

A jettisoned machine gun fell on land owned by Wilkin and Son (Tiptree Jam). It was promptly recovered and put on display in their factory. The Army, on hearing of this, arrived a few days later to confiscate the weapon. However a photograph of the gun can be seen in the Jam Museum.

STOW MARIES

They flew into the sky in the dead of night
To seek out the enemy at great height

Despite the destruction of Zeppelins L32 and L33 (noted in the last chapter) the airborne 'menace' was growing, not only from airships but from the new fixed wing Gotha bombers. The British government responded by requisitioning upwards of 70 sites on farms across eastern England and ordering the rapid building of aerodromes.

120 acres of Flambirds Farm at Stow Maries, near Purleigh, on the Dengie peninsular, was one of the locations chosen. In October 1916 it became the base for six aircraft of the 37 (Home Defence) Squadron's 'B' flight, plus part of the newly created Royal Flying Corps (RFC). The first commanding officer was Lieutenant Claude Alward Ridley. Only 19 years old, he had joined the RFC a year earlier and seen action in France. On one of his missions while flying agents into enemy occupied France, engine trouble with his aircraft forced him to spend three months at large behind enemy lines before eventually making his escape through Belgium and Holland. He was awarded the Military Cross and Distinguished Service Order for his efforts.

With 'B' flight in residence, the first six months of Stow Maries aerodrome witnessed a period of intensive training for air and ground crew. The rest of '37 Squadron', which was charged with the eastern aerial defence of London, was dispersed locally with 'A' flight located at Rochford, 'C' flight at Goldhanger on the north side of the River

Blackwater and with the staff headquarters at Woodham Mortimer six miles away.

The first recorded operational flight took place from Stow Maries on the night of 23rd/24th May 1917 when Claude Ridley (now promoted to Captain) and Lieutenant G Keddie were ordered to intercept a large Zeppelin raid targeting London. No losses were reported although on their return ground crews discovered a number of bullets holes in the aircraft. 'C' Flight took credit for the squadron's first confirmed 'kill' when early on 17th June 1917, 2nd Lieutenant Watkins engaged L48, the last Zeppelin to be shot down in England during the war. As 1917 progressed the air war intensified. Day and night patrols continued and the squadron began to suffer losses caused in the main by pilot inexperience or unreliable aircraft.

In the summer of 1917 'A' Flight moved to Stow Maries effectively doubling the size of the station. Building continued unabated and during 1918 the staff HQ also took up residence. It was not until February 1919, with the war over, that 'C' Flight also moved to Stow Maries, bringing for the first time the whole of 37 Squadron together at one station. Total staffing levels were recorded at around 300 personnel and 24 aircraft. Yet this state of affairs was short lived. The following month 37 Squadron moved to Biggin Hill in Kent, leaving the Stow Maries site empty. The aerodrome was returned to agriculture with the buildings, where possible, being used intermittently for both storage and accommodation purposes.

The Royal Aircraft factory replica BE2 still flying

For many years Stow Maries lay undisturbed and largely forgotten. In 2008 the former aerodrome was purchased by Steve Wilson and Russell Savory. In partnership with English Heritage, Maldon and Essex Councils and the National Heritage Memorial Fund the aerodrome is progressively being restored as a heritage site based on how it looked in 1919.

Based at Stow Maries is a reproduction 'Royal Aircraft Factory BE2e'. The BE stands for Blériot Experimental. Over 3,000 of these aircraft were made during WWI. The site also has a tearoom, shop and museum. For all intents and purposes the aerodrome grass landing strip is operational, all be it only for small aircraft. Stow Maries is described as Europe's most complete largest surviving World War I aerodrome.

MISSING PERSON FROM HARLOW

Old Loftus Arkwright was never the same
When his son went missing - of the same name.
He went from fair Harlow we do not know where,
'Disappeared' on his family tree - if you look for
him there.

The name of Arkwright, inextricably woven into Britain's industrial revolution, is usually associated with the *dark satanic mills* of northern England. Less well known is that for over a hundred years descendants of Sir Richard Arkwright, the inventor of the 'Waterframe' spinning machine, had an association with the Harlow in Essex. This connection ceased with the fifth generation of Arkwrights providing an unsolved mystery, – what happened to Loftus Arkwright?

The Harlow connection began with Sir Richard Arkwright's son, also Richard. Successful like his father, he became one of the richest men in England. His son Joseph, an ordained clergyman, married Anne, a member of the wealthy Wigram family of Walthamstow. Anne's father Sir Robert Wigram suggested to Richard Arkwright that he buy Mark Hall estate, to provide a home for Joseph and Anne, and install Joseph as the vicar of St Mary the Virgin (Now St Mary-at-Latton). Joseph duly became Squire of Latton and Vicar of St Mary's. As well as developing a passion for foxhunting, he expanded the estate which he had inherited on his father's death. Loftus Wigram was the seventh of Joseph's twelve children and shared his father's love of the hunt. He was given the management of Little Parndon Manor, which Joseph had acquired by 1850. A talented farmer, he was the only son to remain at Latton. On Joseph's death in 1864 he inherited the whole estate including Mark Hall.

Loftus Wigram built himself a new house, Parndon Hall, which still stands today, and serves as an education centre for the local Hospital NHS Trust. He became a magistrate and was Master of Foxhounds until breaking his back in a hunting accident. Later, he still followed the hunt but was driven in a light open carriage. He died suddenly in 1899, leaving all the estates to his only son Loftus Joseph.

Loftus Joseph was very much in the Arkwright tradition. He went to Eton and Cambridge and was passionate about hunting. Like his father, he was Master of Foxhounds until a serious accident put an end to his riding days too. In 1894 he married Julia Caldwell, the daughter of his rich American tenant of Mark Hall, and in 1895 their first son, just plain Loftus, was born. Twin brothers Godfrey and John came along in 1901. The Arkwright estates continued to grow under Loftus Joseph. By 1930 he had acquired the manors of Netteswell, Passmores and Canons in Great Parndon and other local properties under the umbrella of the 'Mark Hall Estates Company'. His wife left him in 1919 and Loftus Joseph became increasingly eccentric and reclusive. He was rarely seen in public and died in 1950. He is buried in St Mary's churchyard, Little Parndon.

Traditionally Loftus, the eldest son, would inherit but he had rebelled against generations of Arkwright tradition. Unlike his father, or his twin brothers, he had no interest in hunting, the church, the armed forces or even expanding the Arkwright property empire. At the age of twenty-five, having left the family home to work in a garage, he simply disappeared. This was in 1919, the year of his parent's separation and eventual divorce. Did he change his name and just drop out of circulation, meet with an accident or even emigrate?

Whatever happened he has not been heard of since, although there have been rumours that he lived the life of a hermit in Africa. Since Loftus' brother John had died at sea in 1942 John's twin Godfrey inherited Parndon Hall. He left Parndon after three years and died within six months. The Arkwright Estates were purchased for the Harlow New Town development. The Arkwright name is remembered today in the housing area, 'Arkwrights', in Netteswell.

RADIO 2MT (TWOEMMATOC)

The inventor of radio and wireless,
His genius unrecognised in Rome,
Came to England seeking success
And made Chelmsford his technical home.

Guglielmo Marconi was born in Bologna in 1874 to an Italian father and an Irish mother. At the age of twenty he was experimenting with communicating intelligence without the use of connecting wires. Within two years he had invented the first practical radio-signalling system able to transmit signals over a distance of a few kilometres. He offered his invention to the ministry of posts and telegraphs in Rome but they were not interested. Disappointed, he left Italy for England with his mother in February 1896.

After being introduced to William Preece, the Engineer in Chief at the Post Office, Marconi patented his system and formed the 'Wireless Telegraph and Signal Company Ltd'. Continuing his experiments on the roof of the Post Office Headquarters in London, in 1899 he established communication across the English Channel. In 1901 he successfully communicated between Poldhu in Cornwall and St John's, Newfoundland.

Marconi's company began manufacturing wireless equipment in a former silk mill in Hall Street, Chelmsford. The 'radio factory' flourished and in 1912 a new factory was built in New Street to cope with demand. Eager to explore public entertainment broadcasting, Marconi gained ministerial approval to make an experimental broadcast. This took the form of a concert, sponsored by the *Daily Mail*. It was broadcast from a hastily converted packing shed next to the transmitter hut on the edge of the New Street works. The concert featured the famous soprano Dame Nellie Melba. At seven o'clock on 15th June 1920, after a short delay, Dame Nellie sang. The concert was a great success and was heard clearly wherever there was equipment to receive it.

However, in November 1920, the Post Office, which had a monopoly on communications, suspended broadcasts from Chelmsford on the grounds of 'interference with legitimate services' such as the fledgling air traffic control. The Navy and the Army were also horrified at the prospect of the airways being used for 'entertainment' as this was 'not in the best interests of Imperial defence'. Yet, the clock could not be turned back.

The 'public' clamoured for more. In due course the Postmaster General grudgingly issued licences for further entertainment broadcasts from Marconi's Airborne Telephony Research Department in Writtle using the call sign Two Emma Toc (2MT). Regular transmission began in February 1922. In May a second station, using the call sign 2LO, began broadcasting from the top of London's Marconi House in Aldwych. On the basis of this continuing success the new British Broadcasting Company was formed and public service broadcasting as we know it was born.

Some fourteen years later, in 1936, using an aerial and transmitters designed and made in the New Street factory, the BBC began the first scheduled television service in the world from Alexandra Palace in the River Lea valley.

Guglielmo Marconi died on 20th July 1937. Thousands of mourners lined the streets at his funeral in Rome and transmitters around the world observed a two minutes silence. Although he lived much of his life in England, he never lost touch with his family home. He is buried there in the grounds of the Villa Griffone, at Pontecchio near Bologna.

BERTRAM THE CLOWN

Clown Bertram performed and impressed the boss.
For 18 years the pier never made a loss.

In 1922 Albert Edward Harvey turned up unannounced at the Clacton Pier office of Barney Kingsman and patiently waited to see him. Kingsman had just acquired Clacton Pier and a fleet of ageing passenger vessels, the 'Belles', from the liquidators. Eventually Harvey was shown in where he was gruffly asked, "What do you want boy? Can't you see I'm busy"? Harvey said he was a children's entertainer using the name 'Bertram' and was looking for work. Kingsman thinking "that's all I need" immediately summoned his foreman and barked, "This boy claims to be a children's entertainer so give him a week's trial, then sling him out".

Kingsman sat back and studied the long list of pier repairs outstanding and pondered on how much they would cost. The following afternoon, working in his office, he was disturbed by a huge din coming from outside. Kingsman stormed out to complain only to find an amazing sight. An extract from an interview concerning the pier, in a 1934 edition of the magazine *Tit Bits*, sums up the scene:

'At the end of the pier a thousand people were standing, and scores of children sitting on a bit of carpet, and they were shrieking with laughter, while a young man, aided by a couple of children from the audience, played a burlesque drama…. It was a riot.'

That was the beginning of Clown Bertram. The week's trial was to last for 18 years! The pier had originally opened in 1877 during the great period of Victorian pier building. Its original purpose was to serve as a landing stage for trips for London city dwellers wanting to escape the pollution and grime of the metropolis. The passenger steamers did good business until the arrival of the railways. Then trippers could get to, and return from, Clacton more quickly with the added advantage of not being sea-sick en-route.

At first 'Bertram' performed in the open, then in a specially built theatre accommodating 500 at the pier head. However the audience soon outgrew that too. The old pier pavilion was renamed as the Jollity and its capacity increased to 1,000. This too was frequently full to capacity. Many adults and children would queue for hours to get in. Clown Bertram was the best loved performer ever to appear on Clacton Pier and some famous celebrities to be, such as Jimmy Hanley and Warren Mitchell (Alf Garnett), appeared with Bertram as child amateur performers.

The show had an unbroken run from 1922 to 1939 and unusually for many 'stars' Bertram went out on a high. The outbreak of World War II brought entertainment on the pier to an abrupt end. Clacton was closed for the duration of the war apart from local residents and the military. Bertram never appeared there again. Albert Edward Harvey died at the age of sixty five, happy in the knowledge that he had brought joy to thousands of children.

CRITTALL'S NEW JERUSALEM

Workers could be hired but with nowhere to house them,
What was a keen socialist like Francis Crittall to do?

In October 1849 Francis Berrington Crittall arrived in Braintree and opened an ironmongery business at 27 High Street (now Bank Street). It was here, above the shop in 1860 that his second son Francis Henry was born. On completing his schooling Francis Henry was sent to Birmingham to work for a bedstead maker where he met and married his wife Laura. In 1883 Francis Henry returned to Braintree to take over the shop. Francis was an ambitious and inventive engineer and this small shop, under his control, grew into the global Crittall manufacturing business. It survived for over a hundred years with the Crittall family at the helm. Francis Henry had two sons who were both involved in the business. Valentine George, born in 1884, also became the Labour MP for Maldon and was later created Baron Braintree. The second son, Walter Francis, was born in 1887 and he became the artistic and technical director of the company. Walter was given the nickname 'Pink' as a child and throughout the company was always known as 'Mr Pink'.

The company's breakthrough came in 1900 with the invention of standardised metal window frames. These were to revolutionise the building industry and create huge demand. Employing around 2,000 men at this time, the company was still expanding and was desperately short of housing to accommodate its ever growing work force. Francis Crittall also had a nickname and was known affectionately (throughout the factory) as 'The Guv'nor'. A keen socialist, he held the view that a happy and contented workforce was a productive one. With this in mind he set to solve the accommodation problem.

First he toyed with, and then discarded, the idea of building a housing estate near Braintree. Encouraged by his sons who were also admirers of the 'Garden City' movement, he decided to emulate Titus Salt and George Cadbury and their model villages of Saltaire and Bournville.

On November 3rd 1925 Crittall's purchased, for £7,500, the 200 acre Boars Tye Farms near Silver End on which to build their garden village. There was enough land for a population of seven to eight thousand people. Drainage, water and electricity supplies, all were to be unique to the village. It would contain churches, a school, a cinema, a hotel and its own department store selling food from a company owned farm. It even had its own bus service.

The houses, many designed by 'Mr Pink' who was influenced by the German 'Bauhaus' modernistic style, each had their own garden. They had hot and cold running water which was not found in many homes at that time. The hot water came from the factory's excess capacity. They were built on tree lined avenues, with plenty of public space in the form of gardens and recreational areas. A new factory, commissioned as the house building started, supplied electricity to the residents from its own generators.

The 'Silver End Development Company' was set up to build the village. One of the directors, Captain Reiss, brought his experience as a member of the board of 'Welwyn Garden City' to the project. The style of the village was 'Modern' and one of the few examples seen in Essex. The completion of the Silver End project was overseen by Valentine George. When the village was fully functioning his parents took up residence in 'The Manors', a large detached house where they lived until Francis' death in 1934.

Valentine George was an ardent believer in the welfare state and introduced his principles into the company. He employed people with disabilities at the same rates of pay as anybody else. The conditions of employment were in advance of most and the good relations with the workforce were evidenced by the fact that throughout the general strike in 1926 normal production continued undisturbed. In 1931, in recognition of his efforts in promoting the workers welfare, he was given a knighthood and, in 1947, elevated to the peerage as Baron Braintree. He was also made a director of the Bank of England and had responsibility for transferring the printing of banknotes to the new factory in Debden, Essex.

At its peak Crittall's employed 5,000 people. The company prided itself in being progressive. It opened its permanent sports ground on the Cressing Road in 1923 and was the first major company in Britain to abolish Saturday working in 1926.

In 1968 the Crittall business was bought by Slater Walker Securities and the family connection ended when Walter 'Mr Pink' Crittall retired in 1974. Although the company produced their 50 millionth steel window in 1978, and today Witham is home to Crittall's International business, the late 20th century saw the company's decline from its former success.

HAUNTED HOUSE

Borley Rectory sadly is no more.
A lamp was knocked over on a pile of books
And the days, and nights, of yore
Were gone (or were they?) for the resident spooks.

Borley Church has stood, close to the Suffolk border with commanding views of the River Stour valley, from Saxon times. In 1863, the Reverend Henry Dawson Ellis Bull built a new rectory close to the church to house his growing family. The large brick, castle-like construction was a forbidding building, surrounded by tall trees and subject to peculiar acoustic effects from the wind. It had attics, cellars, several staircases and eleven bedrooms and was a warren of a building. Seventy five years later the rectory was burnt down by the owner, William Gregson. According to insurance investigators it was a deliberate act of arson and a bogus insurance scam.

In the intervening years, largely due to the *Daily Mirror* and the psychic investigator Harry Price, the house gained the reputation of being the most haunted house in England. Even today ghost hunters regularly hold weekend vigils in the grounds of Borley Church. At Halloween and mid-summer larger gatherings of spirit seekers descend upon Borley and the police need to keep a strong presence to maintain order.

Local legend has it that the rectory was built on the site of a 13th century monastery from which a monk eloped with a nun from nearby Bures Convent, escaping in a coach and horses. Soon captured they were brought back and punished. The monk was hanged and the nun bricked up alive in the convent. Although there was never a monastery at Borley there have been many alleged sightings of the couple and a phantom coach and horses. Another tale was of a black clad nun who walked the garden, who it was even claimed had been seen by all four of Bull's daughters in daylight.

When Bull died in 1892 his son Harry took over as rector. He married at the age of 48, much to the disgust of his unmarried sisters who made life unbearable for his young wife. They even accused her of poisoning him when he died in 1927. Harry Bull was eccentric in many ways and firmly believed in the ghost of the phantom nun. He is alleged to have threatened his family that he would return from the grave. In 1928 the new incumbent, the Rev. Eric Smith, and his wife Mabel, arrived.

They were regaled with stories and rumours of strange happenings; footsteps, lights being turned on or off, doorbells ringing and keys disappearing. Whether they were taken in or not is unknown but Eric Smith contacted the *Daily Mirror* who sent a reporter to investigate, together with Harry Price. They reported objects being thrown across rooms, and the reporter claimed to have seen the nun. The Smiths moved out in 1929, but not before Mabel Smith had made detailed notes for her book, *Murder at The Parsonage*, but this was never published.

Lionel Foyster a cousin of the Bulls, took over as rector in 1930 and moved into the rectory with his wife Marianne, twenty-one years his junior. It was during their five year stay that the tales of hauntings really grew. The Foysters, also intended to publish a book (though this also never happened), in which two thousand psychic happenings were recorded. There is suspicion that the 'happenings' were created by Marianne with Lionel's connivance. Harry Price, who was involved with them throughout, had his doubts yet he still described the Foyster's tenure as "The most extraordinary and best documented case of haunting in the annals of psychical research".

The Foysters left Borley Rectory in 1935. Harry Price then leased the building for a year. During this time he recorded objects moving and the sounds of footsteps but nothing comparable to Marianne's earlier claims. The results of his investigations, as well as many of the Foyster's 'happenings', are recorded in his two books, *The Most Haunted House in England* and *The End of Borley Rectory*.

On leaving Borley, Marianne confined Lionel, who was by then a sick old man, to the attic of their new house in Suffolk, at times passing him off as her father. She is reputed to have had a string of affairs at Borley but went even further in Suffolk when she bigamously married a travelling salesman. After Lionel's death Marianne married an American Serviceman and moved to the USA in 1946, where she lived until her death in 1992.

As for the Rectory, it burnt down in 1939 when William Gregson, its last owner, overturned an oil lamp amongst piles of books. Maybe the ghosts perished in the fire? There are those who believe in ghosts whatever the evidence may indicate and for them Borley will no doubt always hold fascination. On the other hand tales of adultery, bigamy, jealously, poisoning and possible murder are subjects which, probably founded in fact, are equally gripping.

HAPPY HARRY

The crowds come and go, as the morning turns to evening.
It's time to go, but let us sing once more:
'I'm H. A. P. P. Y. I'm H. A. P. P. Y.
I'm H. A. P. I'm H. A. P. I'm H. A. P. P. Y.

Happy Harry was a familiar figure to the thousands of people who visited Southend's seafront between 1910 and 1966. An old style evangelist preacher, he took his chance on what was known as Southend's 'Speaker's Corner'. There was competition from other speakers representing the Salvation Army, the Exclusive Brethren, the Elim Church and the political parties. As Harry put it, "Marine Parade was like a lunatic asylum at weekends". It was his happy revivalist singing and preaching that drew the big crowds. He attracted dozens, and on occasion hundreds, of people to listen spellbound by the rain shelter on Marine Parade.

Happy Harry's real name was the Reverend George Wood. He had spent a year at Bible College before being ordained as a minister in the Pioneer Pentecostal Church in 1909. Two years later he was called to preach in Southend. It was through his efforts that the first Pentecostal Church in Southend was opened in Clarence Road in 1919. Rev. Wood preached there for eighteen months and was paid £12 per month. Apart from this, he relied upon the generosity of his audience on the seafront for his sole income.

A preacher first and foremost, Harry was also a natural entertainer and the crowds loved him. He was not a big man, he would stand on a folding chair, or sometimes just on the pavement, and sing out in a voice that belied his smallish frame.

There's something more than gold my friend, there's something more than gold
to know your sins are all forgiven, is something more than gold.

This would soon attract an audience. It would be followed with a story from the gospel delivered in Harry's inimitable style, more singing, then finish with what, for many, became his theme song:-

'It's rolling in, it's rolling in. The sea of love is rolling in.
I believe that I receive, The sea of love that's rolling in.' etc.,

This chorus was a signal for his audience to roll pennies and halfpennies towards Harry. On one occasion a man was heard to shout

"Here y'are Harry, here's a penny, give us a ha'p'ny change". And Harry did. It was this sort of action, done with a smile, that endeared him to many as much as his preaching.

However some people made his life a misery and at times their abuse got out of hand. When people rolled coins to him, occasionally young children would run in and pinch them before Harry could pick them up, and there was always heckling. These things he could meet with a smile. Hooligan nastiness appeared at times when young men would heat up pennies with cigarette lighters to burn Harry's fingers when he picked them up. Once they tied newspaper to his coat tail and set fire to it.

Sometimes things were so bad that police were called to break-up rowdy onlookers. Harry was once lifted bodily by two men who would have thrown him in the sea had it not been for the intervention of some of his audience. In another incident he took a blow to the face which smashed his glasses, leading to the loss of sight in one eye. His attacker was fined two pounds! It is said that some of the most hurtful abuse he received was from conservative Christian elements that hated his Pentecostal movement.

None of this deterred Harry from his preaching. His devotion to religion led to his separation from his wife (although they were together again in 1960) and estrangement from his son. He said of this, "I regret hurting them but I am happy, I have seen thousands of converts to the Pentecostal Church".

In 1938 Happy Harry was admitted to Runwell Mental Hospital. On his 'release' he stood for election as an independent candidate for Southend Borough Council. He put on his election address that 'I am the only candidate who has been certified sane'.

During World War Two, Harry worked for the War Office and remained there as a messenger until 1954. Although never in good health, he still preached regularly after work and at weekends, not only in Southend, but also in London and as far as Bedfordshire.

In 1966, his health failing, Harry moved to an old folk's home in Streatham, south London. In 1972, 'The Hot Gospelling Rev. George Wood,' was brought to Southend by the *Evening Echo* to relive his memories, 'of crowds of people singing and praying and his own voice thundering out urging them to a better way of life'. 'Happy Harry' died in 1974. He is remembered by a plaque erected by the Southend Society, situated on the sea wall opposite Pleasant Road.

TWO SISTERS, TWO CHURCHES

From birth they wanted everything they touched.
Each fighting for anything the other one clutched.

Willingale is a small village lying between Ongar and Chelmsford. Its population is about 450. It has two churches, Willingale Spain and Willingale Doe. It is unusual for such a small community to have two same faith churches and it is extremely rare for both churches to be built on the same plot of land next door to each other!

One of the explanations for Willingale's churches' side by side existence was that each served to accommodate the spiritual needs of two rival sisters. This supposition is mentioned in area guide books and can be traced back to the Victorians. With the passage of time more detail has come to light, or alternatively the story has been embellished.

The two sisters in question were of Saxon descent called Beornia and Synnove. A year apart in age, they were daughters of Rheda and Aeschere, a noble knight. From the time the sisters were first able to communicate they bickered. Initially they argued over playthings or food but then it was clothes, their tutor or the attention received from their parents. As they developed into young women they fought for the affections of Tristram, son of Hew Rhyddol, a Norman landowner. Relations between the Saxons and the Normans were fractious at the best of times. To spite her sister Synnove provoked a fierce argument between Tristram and her father which got out of hand and resulted in both men's deaths. The sisters could not even find solace in their shared grief so their mother Rheda financed the building of a second church to enable them to pray separately for redemption. Plausible though this legend is, the archaeological evidence shows that the churches were built approximately 200 years apart. The first church, Willingale Spain, was built after the Norman Conquest under the patronage of Hervey D'Espania. Also known as D'Ispania he came over with William the Conqueror and was responsible for Spain's Hall near Finchingfield.

In about 1320 the D'Ou family arrived in Willingale. They were wool merchants. Wool and cloth were expanding industries in early 14th century Essex and probably the biggest employers after agriculture. As the local population increased, the church was not large enough to accommodate the worshippers.

Rather than pull it down and build a larger one the D'Ou family built a second church, Willingale Doe, beside Willingale Spain and on land already consecrated. A new parish was created which gave the village a second priest. In 1929 the two churches were united again. However Willingale Spain fell into disuse and became a virtual ruin. It was restored in the 1950s by the *Friends of Friendless Churches* although it still has no electricity. Today both churches fall within the parish of Willingale with Shellow and Berners Roding, all of them sharing the same priest.

Two Churches side by side in Willingdale

It is possible that the two sisters lived in the 1320s when the second church was built. In that case the argument that resulted in the deaths of a suitor and the father of the sisters could have happened. Willingale Doe could have been built to keep the grieving sisters apart. However the Saxon connection is only relevant during the eleventh century, the time of the building of the first church, when there was a real divide between the victorious Normans and the defeated Saxons. By the fourteenth century this had disappeared and a new national identity was taking shape - Englishness.

'HISTORY IS BUNK'

'History is Bunk', so Henry Ford said,
It means nothing we don't want tradition.

"History is more or less bunk". So said Henry Ford in an interview with Charles Wheeler for the *Chicago Tribune* on May 25th, 1916. Yet history shows that Ford has made a significant contribution to the development of the small Essex town of Dagenham.

Ford had been producing the 'Model T' since 1913 at Trafford Park, Manchester. After the 'Great War' demand was such that to meet it a new factory was needed. The nation-wide search for a site finally settled on Dagenham riverside where Samuel Williams owned much of the land. His company's development of Dagenham dock, providing shipping access together with good road and rail links, made it an ideal site. In 1924 Ford bought five hundred acres from Samuel Williams and the 'Ford Dagenham Car Plant' was under way.

In 1928 Henry Ford decided to come and inspect the new project. He and his wife, Clara, set sail for England, travelling incognito as Mr and Mrs Robinson, maybe to avoid publicity, since, though highly successful, Henry Ford was not universally popular. While here he met King George V and Queen Mary and the leading politicians of the day.

Henry, impressed with the new project, appointed Sir Percival Perry to re-launch 'Ford Britain' as the hub of his

The First off the Line

new European organisation. In December 1929 Ford Motor Company Limited (UK) was floated and work on the new Dagenham factory started.

When production began in 1931, two thousand workers and their families were brought on special trains from Manchester to their new homes in Dagenham. Many more were hired locally. On October the first 1931, the Managing Director, Roland Hill, drove the first vehicle off the assembly line, a Fordson AA truck.

During the forties, due to the importance of Ford's war effort, workers needed permission to leave, even to join the forces. By 1951, despite post war shortages, the new 'Consul and Zephyr' range came into production and Ford was employing upwards of forty thousand people. By 1996 ten million vehicles had been built at Dagenham since production started in 1931. The names of some of the cars - Anglia, Cortina, Capri, Sierra and Mondeo were all famous in their day and the name Ford is inextricably linked with the history of modern Dagenham.

Car production ceased in Dagenham on 20th February 2002 - the last vehicle off the line was a Ford Fiesta. Powered by wind turbines, the plant now contains Ford's designated centre of excellence for the design and manufacture of diesel engines which employs over 2,000 people. The finished engines are exported to plants all over the world.

It is interesting to note that Henry Ford was keen on recycling back in 1930. He decreed that his Dagenham power station should burn the rubbish dumped locally by the London County Council (LCC) - approximately 2,000 tons a week. Apparently the arrangement stopped in 1939 when the LCC demanded payment for its rubbish.

The Last off the Line

PLOTLANDERS

From London to Dunton they came, a trickle then a rush
Seeking respite from the overcrowded, noisy, smoky city crush.
Whole families wanting a weekend retreat or holiday home
Came to the countryside where it was clean and free to roam.

Although, in late Victorian times London was a dirty, grimy city and heavily polluted, it was nevertheless expanding and confident. A new class was emerging. This was not the land owning gentry and certainly not the desperate city poor. This new class consisted of bank workers, skilled artisans, civil servants, merchants, teachers and managers. In recent times they might be called the middle class. They had a measure of job security, a roof over their heads and above all some disposable income.

At the same time conditions in the countryside were anything but rosy. Since 1870 farming had been depressed. Farms were going bankrupt with the land virtually unsaleable. Food was increasingly imported from abroad and much of the land was deemed unsuitable for farming. A report to a Royal Commission in 1898 described a large portion of Essex farming land 'not fit for purpose'. Subsequently recommendations were made that the land be sold off, not as whole farms but in small units or plots. Almost immediately the property developers of the day realised the financial potential and the 'plotlands' scheme was born.

Areas of land, roughly from Laindon to Dunton and north to Billericay were offered for sale. The average size of a plot was 20ft X 160ft and it was offered for sale at £5.00 a plot. An acre could be bought for £30.00 but there were few takers. Plots were marketed to Londoners as, 'land in the countryside - in fresh clean air'. They were also described as, 'the ideal weekend or holiday retreat for hard working town folk'. To begin with take up was slow but it grew steadily, and although interrupted by the First World War, reached a frenzied peak in the early 1930s. The salesmen used all sorts of persuasive inducements in what were known as the 'Champagne sales'. Prospective buyers were offered free or discounted return rail trips from London, lunches and of course champagne to seal a sale.

The new owners took to their acquisitions with gusto. At weekends the Laindon countryside was packed with Londoners engaged in the new fad of DIY. All types of temporary buildings and shacks sprang up with quaint names such as Daisy Dene, Cosy Nook and Lilliville. Lorries, vans and even old railway carriages were converted. Building materials and furniture arrived by any means available, even motorcycle. On Sunday nights the platform at Laindon station was often packed eight deep, for its whole length, with weekenders waiting to catch the last train back to London.

The sudden influx of people living on the plotlands brought problems as at first there was no mains water, no drainage and no sewerage facilities. Water was laid on to properties closest to the station and a series of standpipes were erected. The local council, Billericay, became somewhat alarmed, not only about the provision of water but at the state of some of the homes that were erected. Several prosecutions were issued over the haphazard construction of some dwellings.

During the Second World War many people used their plotland homes as refuges from the London Blitz. This was no guarantee of safety since enemy aircraft used the Thames as a guide to London. They could be shot down and crash nearby. Damaged planes often jettisoned their bombs and unspent ammunition over the area.

After World War II, much of the capital lay in ruins. There was a desperate need to re-house many Londoners. One of the solutions to this was to create the new town of Basildon. Post-war recreational tastes were changing and interest in plotland sites waned. Caravan parks were springing up and holiday camps were booming. Most plotland sites were cleared by the New Town Corporation to satisfy the huge demand for housing. The clearing continued until 1980. Today a substantial green area of plotland remains as the Langdon Nature Reserve run by The Essex Wildlife Trust. Close to the entrance to the park is 'The Havens', an 'original' plotland dwelling that serves as a museum.

WHERE IS ZLIN?

People flocked to Tilbury on hearing the news
Thomas Bata needed people to make his shoes.

Zlin lies 1,000 miles from Essex, in the south-eastern corner of the Czech Republic, close to Vienna and Budapest. A large wall map displayed in the Bata Resource Centre in East Tilbury shows Zlin at the centre of the world. It was the birthplace of Thomas Bata who created the Bata Shoe Company.

Bata founded his company in 1894 and his dream was to make cheap affordable shoes for everyone. He also wanted shoes to be made in modern clean factories by a contented workforce that enjoyed good pay and welfare conditions. Back in Victorian times owning a good pair of shoes was a luxury and once acquired they were expected to last a lifetime. Working conditions were grim, with virtually no health or safety regulations and little sickness care or pension provision.

Bata was not a utopian idealist. He was a businessman who believed that a happy worker was a productive one. This philosophy had been proven in the Zlin factory. To further his ambition to be the 'shoemaker to the world' he chose East Tilbury, Essex as the site for his factory in the UK. It would not be just a factory but a self-sufficient community on the original Zlin model. Work started in 1932 under the direction of Czech architects Vladimir Karfik and Frantizek Gahura. Everything was built as seen in a normal town – an hotel, a cinema, restaurants, a dance hall, sports facilities, a garage, and shops including a shoe shop. The community would even have its own newspaper *The Bata Record*. Everything, however, was owned by Bata.

Production began in 1933 but Thomas Bata never lived to see shoes coming off the production line in East Tilbury. He was killed in a plane crash a year earlier. His half-brother, Dr. Jan Bata, took over the helm at the company.

The arrival of the Bata Company in Essex aroused many misgivings. Like most countries, Britain was suffering from economic depression and mass unemployment following the Wall Street Crash. 'Foreigners' coming to Britain to set up factories and telling the British how to run them caused alarm. The press carried several reports reflecting these sentiments. Doubts were expressed about the new welding techniques used in the structure of the factory. There was criticism too of the fact that there would be Czech foremen supervising locals. A number of letters were also published about boys (the Bata Boys), some as young as 14, being sent off to Czechoslovakia to train for up to three years. In those days foreign travel was almost unknown except for the colonial service, the military or the privileged few.

It was the fear of the new and the different that caused most of these concerns. Gradually Bata overcame resistance to their presence and their way of operating, despite a prolonged strike about union recognition in 1937. Yet through all the difficulties in the first few years, people travelled from all over the county, often on foot or bicycle, to seek work with Bata.

The company benefits for workers were previously unknown, certainly in East Tilbury. Housing was provided for families and young unmarried workers were often accommodated in the company hotel or hostels. High standards had to be maintained and discipline was rigid. Even the state of the gardens was regularly checked.

On arrival workers were greeted with rousing music at the factory gates to welcome them in. However, lateness or slacking on the job was not tolerated. On dismissal not only the job would go but the house too. The Bata's management did their level best to create a cult feeling of loyalty to the company.

Towards the end of the 1930s the dark clouds of the Second World War were looming and those senior members of the Bata family still in Czechoslovakia fled to England, the USA or Canada. The war gave a boost to production and the factory turned out thousands of military boots. After the war the Bata Family remained in exile as the new communist masters in Eastern Europe nationalised all the factories. Thomas Bata junior did not return to his homeland until the end of the Soviet era in 1989.

For a time Bata was one of Britain's biggest exporters. Over 3,000 people worked on site. The machine-age logic that created both Zlin and East Tilbury was the seed of their demise. Continuing technical innovation required fewer people. General industrial malaise in Britain in the 1970s and stiff competition from Europe, and then the Far East, hastened the end. The last shoes were made in East Tilbury in 2006. Since 1993 the factory and estate housing provided by the company for its employees have been part of a designated conservation area. A bronze statue of Thomas Bata stands outside the front of the old factory building.

LITTLE SHIPS OF LEIGH

'Defender, Endeavour, Letitia
Reliant, Renown and Resolute :-
Were the little ships sent from Leigh
They had to join 800 more
To sail to Dunkirk's distant shore
And change a course of history.'

May 1940. Hitler's armies had marched through Holland and Belgium and were sweeping across France. The British Expeditionary Force (BEF) and the French forces retreated and were cut off. A German spearhead reached the sea, leaving the allied forces trapped in a small area of coast around Dunkirk.

On the 26th May a contingency plan to evacuate the troops, code named 'Operation Dynamo', was swiftly put into action by the admiralty. On May 30th, from Southend pier, requisitioned by the Navy as *HMS Leigh*, requests were made for volunteer crews and their shallow draft vessels to help in the exercise.

The response from the fishermen of Leigh was immediate. Arthur Dench was the first to report with his boat *Letitia*. He was quickly joined by five other Leigh cockle boats, the *Defender, Endeavour, Reliance, Renown* and *Resolute*, and their crews. These six boats, under the overall control of Sub-Lieutenant Solomon RN, left Southend Pier at 11:00 am on the 31st May bound for Dunkirk. Although coming under attack from German bombers, they arrived at close to seven in the evening and promptly set about ferrying stranded troops from the beach to the larger ships anchored in deeper waters.

The Leigh Bawleys with their broad beam and flattish bottoms, designed to cope with the Thames estuary sandbanks, were ideally suited for this work. The ships averaging only thirty feet in length and ten feet wide, between them they rescued many thousands of soldiers. In fact the total rescued by the armada of small boats commandeered for this operation was in excess of three hundred thousand.

In the early hours of June 1st the Leigh men started for home. The *Renown* had developed engine trouble and at 1:15 am hailed the *Letitia* who took her in tow. Thirty-five minutes later, as Arthur Dench recalled "A terrible explosion took place, the *Renown* had hit a mine and a hail of wood splinters came down on our deck. In the pitch dark we could do nothing except pull in the tow-rope, which was just as we had passed it out to the *Renown* three-quarters of an hour before. But not a sign of the *Renown*".

The rest of the Leigh boats continued to Ramsgate then on to Leigh where they were met by their families waiting at the waterside.

Arthur Dench said of the Renown's crew, "They knew nothing of war. They went to save, not to fight..... It was a small tragedy in the great disaster of those days of war yet great in the hearts of Leigh people".

On June 4th a letter of appreciation from Naval Control to Sidney Ford of Leigh read, "The ready willingness with which seamen from every walk of life came forward to assist their brother seamen of the Royal Navy will not be forgotten".

In May 1968 these events were commemorated at St Clements Church by a plaque and flags being dedicated in the Chapel of the Resurrection. In 1972, in the churchyard, a memorial was erected to the Fishermen of Leigh, and specifically Frank and Leslie Osborne, Harry Noakes and Harold Graham Porter, the crew of the *Renown*.

The *Endeavour* is the only surviving Leigh boat of those that went to Dunkirk. Registered with the 'Association of Dunkirk Little Ships', has now been extensively restored. The *Endeavour,* along with other 'little ships' has has made a number of return trips to Dunkirk to mark anniversaries of operation 'Dynamo'. On all occasions the vessels and crews have returned unscathed.

STRIKING BACK

After the dark days of forty one,
There was a job that needed to be done.
No longer just defending the land
Taking the fight to the enemy was planned.

On the Dengie peninsular, not far from Maldon, the old Magnox towers over the banks of the River Blackwater. This was Britain's first commercial nuclear power station and is built on the site of an old RAF airfield – Bradwell Bay. The airfield became operational in April 1942 when the Second World War was in its third year. Slowly the tide of battle was turning in favour of the allied cause. The threat of invasion to the British Isles had receded and there was an increasing determination to take the fight to the enemy.

The first arrivals at Bradwell were Canadians manning a squadron of twin-engine Boston aircraft painted in matt black. These aircraft were used as intruders for night operations over occupied Europe. Soon after, there followed a British mosquito squadron employed to attack specific enemy targets in France. As the war progressed many more squadrons came and went, or were rotated through, as the allies advanced after D Day. During the airfield's life, apart from the British and Canadians, New Zealanders, Australians and Czechs were based there.

A whole variety of ancillary missions were undertaken such as pathfinding, bomber escort and troop carrier support, the latter especially for the D-Day landings and the airborne landings at Arnhem in Holland. Of vital importance was the airfield's role in Air Sea Rescue. Returning aircraft were often forced to ditch in the sea. Sometimes they just ran out of fuel before reaching land. Homecoming Halifax and Lancaster bombers would also use Bradwell Bay as an emergency landing site because of its close proximity to the coast. The last operation from Bradwell was in April 1945 and the airfield closed completely in December that year.

An impressive cast iron replica 'Mosquito' is the centrepiece of the memorial which stands on the corner of the original site. One hundred and twentyone aircrew were lost flying from Bradwell Bay. A stone displays the names of the missing flyers with the legend:-

'who in answer to the call of duty
left the airfield to fly into the blue forever'.

MULBERRY

Trips around the Mulberry and tales of yesteryear
That sailor men have told to me whilst holding back a tear.

Just over one mile from Thorpe Bay's shore, in the Thames, a 2,500 ton concrete Phoenix caisson lays partially sunk in the mud. It is a section of the Mulberry Harbour destined for use after the D Day landings in World War Two. *Operation Overlord*, the invasion of Europe by 250,000 allied soldiers, took place on the 6th June 1944. It was an unprecedented logistical challenge. It was assumed that all the major French ports would be unusable which meant the allies needed to take their own harbours with them to support the landings and to re-supply the troops once ashore.

Most of the caissons were built in and around docks on the River Thames. Each concrete caisson was hollow and if made watertight would float, although it is difficult to imagine concrete caissons weighing up to 5,000 tons bobbing about on the high seas. The plan was to tow them to the site of the proposed harbour location on the Normandy coast and sink them in position. They would then serve as supports for the landing bridges.

The section resting in the River Thames was not made locally. It was one of six built in Goole dry docks, on the River Humber, by Henry Boot and Company. Classed as C1s these were the smallest of the caissons. One of them, while being moved south, sprang a leak off the River Crouch. It was towed into the Thames Estuary to await inspection but in a squall it broke free and ran aground. The concrete shell was punctured, flooding it. At low tide it settled and broke in two which made it impossible to recover. Building the caissons was a huge task and undertaken in great secrecy.

An apprentice Frank Agar, who worked on the project for four months, commented that the workers had no idea what they were building. Some speculated they were concrete barges! Apart from the 500 people employed on building the six made in Goole another 6,000 worked on them in Essex. The name Mulberry was not significant, simply a code word for harbour and one of numerous code words originating during the war. The concrete caissons were coded Phoenix. A fleet of ocean-going tugs towed them to Normandy after D-Day. Two harbours were built, the first just off Arromanches supporting the British and Canadian sector and the second at Omaha Beach for the Americans.

HORSE PAINTER EXTRAORDINAIRE

After studying in Paris Munnings moved to Cornwall,
When war intervened he responded to the call.
As Canada's artist he painted at the front line of war,
Faithfully recording the scenes that he saw.

Sir Alfred Munnings, who is perhaps England's best known equine artist, bought Castle House in Dedham in 1919, where he lived until his death in 1959. The house is now a museum dedicated to his life and work. In 1944 Munnings was knighted on being elected President of The Royal Academy of Art. With his reputation at an all-time high his work was in great demand.

Five years later however, having served a successful presidential term, his reputation was to take a severe nosedive; Munning's standing plummeted after his valedictory speech at a dinner held in his honour, at the Royal Academy. The speech was broadcast live by the BBC and millions of listeners heard Munnings attacking modernism. Sounding slightly drunk, he dismissed modernist painters such as Cezanne, Picasso and Matisse as 'foolish daubers who had corrupted art'. He went on to relate that Winston Churchill, who was sat next to him, once asked him, "Alfred if you met Picasso coming down the street would you join me in kicking his......something, something". To which Munnings replied, "Yes sir I would". This speech had a disastrous effect on Munning's reputation. He was distinctly out of favour for many years and demand for his work faded. Not until the 1980s did his contribution to art began to be reassessed and currently his paintings attract high prices.

Born in Mendham, Suffolk in 1878, Munning's artistic talents blossomed while apprenticed to Page Brothers, lithographers, in Norwich. Later he studied in Paris at Julian's Academy and also attended Frank Calderon's School of Animal Painting in Finchingfield. His love of horses, both to ride and paint, would become a lifelong passion.

In 1910 Munnings moved to Newlyn in Cornwall to join an artist community in Lamorna. There he became infatuated with Florence Carter-Wood and they were married in 1912. However, the marriage was a disaster which ended with Florence's suicide in 1914. A film, *Summer in February*, adapted from a novel by Jonathan Smith, exploring this period in his life, was released in 2013. Munnings however never ever referred to it himself, even in his three volume autobiography.

During WW1, though not judged fit for active service, Munnings worked close to the front line as a war artist for the Canadian forces. Two of his most notable paintings from this period are a mounted portrait of General Jack Seely Warrior (now in the National Gallery of Canada, Ottawa) and the 'Charge of Flowerdew's Squadron' in what is known as 'the last great cavalry charge', which took place on 30th March 1918, at the Battle of Moreuil Wood to the south east of Amiens in France.

On Munning's death his second wife, Violet, who he married in 1920, decided to devote Castle House to his memory by establishing a museum to display those pictures which were still in her possession. She set up the Violet Munnings Trust Fund after Castle House opened to the public in 1961. Later the Castle House Trust came into existence as a charitable organisation. The ownership of the house, its furnishings and Sir Alfred's paintings, together with some 40 acres of surrounding land and an endowment fund, were vested in the Trustees. The museum is normally open from 1st April to 31st October, Wednesday to Sunday and bank holidays, 2pm-5pm.

Alfred Munnings at work in his heyday

DOWN THE RIVER LEA

Legend has it that when the Danes
Sailed up the river and landed,
King Alfred and a few of his Thanes
Blocked its flow and left them stranded.

The River Lea rises at Leagrave Marsh in Luton, Bedfordshire, 52 miles (83kms) from where it joins the Thames at Bow. In the 9th century the river formed the natural boundary of the Kingdom of the East Saxons. *The Anglo-Saxon Chronicles* record that King Alfred the Great trapped a great Viking force in the upper reaches of the river in 895 after blocking the waterway; allegedly somewhere near Tottenham lock. The Lea remained the dividing line between Essex and London until local government reorganisation in the mid-1960s.

As London grew and prospered many of its industries were moved from the centre to make way for grand housing and places of business. Tanners, slaughterhouses and workshops, producing too much noise, effluent or smell, were the first to be pushed away from fashionable Westminster and outside the city walls to the east. As the industrial revolution gathered pace the Lea valley was seen as an ideal place for industry to flourish. Here land was cheap, transport easy, boats brought raw materials in and goods out. Also waste products could be dumped in the river and washed out to sea. This practice made the River Lea, from Hackney to Bow, one of the most polluted rivers in the country and partially led to cholera outbreaks in east London that killed thousands of people in the nineteenth century. Even as late as 1960, White Post Lane, which once crossed the river at Hackney Wick, was dubbed 'Smelly Lane' by local people due to odours created by nearby factories and the stench coming from the river.

In the last two hundred years the Lea Valley has been a hive of industrial activity. Almost everything connected to the modern industrial world has at some time been manufactured here including ships, railway locomotives, vehicle engines, telecommunications equipment, copying machines, matches and armaments. In 1804 William Congreve manufactured rockets in a factory on a site now occupied by the Bromley-by-Bow gas works. These rockets, used with limited success in the Peninsular War, were probably the first tactical surface to surface missiles. Upstream the famous Lee Enfield rifle, the standard issue in the British army for 60 years, was designed and manufactured at the Royal Small Arms Factory at Enfield Lock. 'Lee' was the designer's name and nothing to do with the river!

After the Second World War demand for household electrical goods grew exponentially. Lea Valley companies such as MK Electric, Belling, Thorne and Ferguson met the demand and became household names. Innovations in valves, transistors and the use of plastics in electronics resulted from pioneering research in the Lea Valley. It was from Alexandra Palace, on the western banks of the river, that the world's first public television broadcast took place at 3pm on the 2nd November 1936.

By 1990 most industries had abandoned the Lea Valley. The great Temple Mills railway hub was a shadow of its former self. Then in 2005 the area was earmarked for major regeneration in order to host the 30th Olympiad', (i.e., 2012 Olympic Games), and the Fourteenth Paralympic Games. By 2012 the Lea Valley had been transformed. In the summer of that year the new Olympic Park at Stratford became home to the great majority of the sporting events, as well as the athletes' village and a giant media centre. The main olympic athletics stadium was the scene of the spectacular opening and closing ceremonies for both games.

The Queen Elizabeth Park, as it is now called, is set to be the lasting legacy of the Olympic Games. Many of the sporting venues will remain, though somewhat modified for public use and the Olympic Stadium is to be the new home of West Ham United Football Club. One of the park's more unusual features, not a sporting venue, is a huge steel sculpture; the *Arcelor Mittal Orbit*, an observation tower located between the main stadium and the aquatics centre. At 115 metres (377 ft) high it is claimed to be Britain's largest piece of public art.

ARMAGEDDON

Into the bowels of the earth
Went the six hundred, the chosen few.

On the A128, between Brentwood and Ongar, prominent signs can be seen with directions to the 'Secret' Nuclear Bunker. It might be more accurate if the signs read; 'This way to the Nuclear Bunker that is no longer secret'. The bunker is one of the more unusual tourist attractions in Essex.

In 1952, officials from the War Office turned up at the Kelvedon Hatch farm of Jim Parrish with a compulsory purchase order for 25 acres of his land. Almost immediately public access to the site was banned and local roads were closed. The site was fenced off and patrolled by armed guards. The first contractor arrived to excavate a huge hole. This was followed by a succession of builders all working under the cloak of the Official Secrets Act. Secrecy was paramount, each group completed their allocated task and left. None of them knew what anyone else was doing or what the final objective of their labour was. Work commenced on 1st October 1952 and having worked nonstop throughout the dark winter months the bunker was completed by the following March.

The only visible evidence was a quite ordinary looking bungalow. Underneath this, and going down 100 feet, was a three-story bunker encased by 10 feet thick reinforced concrete walls. The entrance was shielded by steel blast proof doors weighing one and half tons each. It was hoped the bunker and its inhabitants could survive the force of a close proximity nuclear explosion.

The originally purpose of the bunker was to serve as a ROTOR station. ROTOR was a government code word used to describe the upgrading of air defences at the inception of the Cold War. The Kelvendon Hatch location was one of a number built on the East Coast of the British Isles. The Marconi Company installed in each bunker the most up to date radar and communications equipment available.

As the Cold War intensified and the Soviet Union acquired nuclear weapons, the British Government began to plan how the nation would cope with a nuclear war and its aftermath. The role of the bunker was changed to that of Regional Government Headquarters, with the code name RGHQ 5.1. £10 million was spent on modifications. In the event of a nuclear attack, the bunker would serve as the control centre for London and the surrounding area.

Within it 600 key personnel would be lodged. They would include top civil servants, cabinet ministers and even the Prime Minister of the day. The bunker was fully self-sufficient with its own power supply and water and food for  three months. There was also a 2,500-line telephone exchange and a BBC radio studio that could broadcast to the nation's survivors. A series of civil defence films were made to explain how the population at large should prepare for nuclear war. Most of these were never shown, on the grounds that they might cause panic. If the bomb dropped, scientists in the bunker would monitor fallout and radiation levels and advise on the risks. It was assumed, although millions of people would die, millions would live. Yet many of the living would have a short life expectancy due to severe burns, radiation sickness and lack of medical attention or even starvation. There was no provision to take family members into the bunker. The unit was to be protected by guards outside who would keep unwanted intruders out, and just as important, keep the key personnel in. Just how the guards were to survive is unclear!

In 1989 the Berlin Wall came down and two years later the Soviet Union began to break up. The Government decided the bunker was no longer needed. In December 1994 ownership of the land, including the bunker, reverted to the Parrish family. They have preserved the bunker as a historical reminder of what may have been.

During its 'operational' lifetime when nuclear Armageddon was a distinct possibility there were just two ways to get in or out of the bunker - the entrance tunnel or the emergency stairs at the rear. With the Cold War over and since becoming a tourist 'attraction' a third exit has been added - on the grounds of health and safety!

THE GREAT SURGE

With night, the surge increased the further south it travelled.
On reaching Essex one by one the sea defences unravelled.

At 9.46am on Saturday 31st January 1953 the *Princess Victoria*, a

British Railways car ferry on a routine crossing between Stranraer and Larne in Northern Ireland, sent the following message:- "Hove-to. Vessel not under command. Urgent assistance required".

At 10:32 an SOS was transmitted. The order to abandon ship followed. Shortly afterwards the vessel was overwhelmed and sank. One of the lifeboats too capsized in the mountainous seas. In all 130 passengers and crew perished.

Four hundred miles further south on Canvey Island in Essex, news of the disaster was slow to filter through. Televisions were a novelty and the telephone a luxury. Although the sinking was the top story on radio, details were sketchy. The 24-hour breaking news we know today was then unknown. Those who had heard about the disaster, whilst shocked and saddened, carried on as normal. That same Saturday brought storm force winds and rough seas but nothing out of the ordinary. After all it was mid-winter. The 31st January was to be a great occasion for Canvey Island with the opening of the War Memorial Hall on the High Street by the Deputy Lieutenant of Essex. A brass plaque to the 57 islanders killed in the Second World War was to be unveiled. It was a grand event to celebrate the successful fund-raising effort that had made the hall possible. As the Canvey Islanders prepared for the celebrations, unbeknown to them, a huge depression was moving around Scotland into the North Sea. (Depressions lower air pressure and cause the sea level to rise.) Rising water levels were in turn pushed southwards by winds, now hurricane force. With a record spring tide adding to the surge, an ever-growing wall of water was being forced down the narrowing funnel of the North Sea that separates England from the continental land mass to its narrowest point at the Dover straits.

Along England's East Coast, from early evening, one by one sea defences began to unravel. Yet the people of Essex were oblivious to the unfolding catastrophe as there was no co-ordinated sea defence warning system. While people were being drowned in their homes further up the coast, in Harwich cinemagoers patiently queued in the cold and wind for the next performance at the Electric Cinema, yards from the seafront. At Southend a dance was taking place on the pier head with the water rising all around, lapping right up to the boards.

The surge first hit Essex at Harwich. The sea acted as if under military command. Where it couldn't batter down defences it simply rose up and rolled over them. By midnight Harwich was besieged from three sides with water pouring in and flooding the town. Further south, the holiday village of Jaywick, just south of Clacton, was assaulted in similar fashion. When the water broke through most residents had gone to bed. They were then woken by a tremendous noise and on opening their front doors to investigate water crashed in.

In the Thames Estuary, by 2.00am, Canvey Island had suffered at least 40 breaches to the sea defences. The Islanders were literally fighting for their lives in the pitch dark. The surge raced on up the River Thames flooding vast industrial areas. The whole of Tilbury was flooded and even at Westminster the river came perilously close to breaking over the embankments. As the water retreated it left a devastating trail of death and destruction. People were left marooned and traumatised. There were enormous amounts of material damage. Farm animals had died in their thousands and the soil had been ruined. However the fury was not over. On leaving English shores the surge built up again and struck Holland with renewed savagery inflicting widespread damage and claiming over 1,800 lives. Back on Canvey, within days the whole of the Island was evacuated and remained so for months. On Saturday 31st January 1953, Canvey Islanders were proudly saluting the memory of the ultimate sacrifice paid from five long years of war. It is difficult to believe that within five hours of midnight that figure had been exceeded by the lives lost to the flood on the island alone.

CREATED IN ESSEX
FLYING INTO HISTORY.

Eagle eyed film buffs watching the third James Bond Film, Goldfinger, released in 1964, will have seen secret agent 007 follow the villainous Auric Goldfinger and his henchman Oddjob from a golf course in Kent to Southend Airport, making use of what appears to be an early form of satellite navigation. At Southend Airport, Goldfinger's Rolls Royce was duly loaded on to an aircraft for Geneva, with James Bond and his gadget laden Aston Martin following in hot pursuit on the next flight.

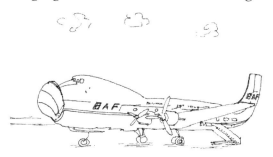 Clearly seen in the background of the film shot is the control tower at Southend Airport. The aircraft in the clip was a British United Air Ferries Carvair, leased to United Artists who made the film.

The Carvair was a product of Essex based Aviation Traders Limited (ATL), a company formed by the low cost flight pioneer Freddy Laker. Designed at Southend and built at the Southend and Stansted workshops, only 21 Carvairs were made. The name was simply a contraction of the three words car - via – air, which neatly sums up why the aircraft came into being. The aircraft was designed to carry up to five cars and 20 passengers or 2-3 cars and 55 passengers.

Although the Carvair was 'made' in Essex the base airframe was a Douglas DC4, built in either Chicago or Orlando. DC4s had seen service as cargo or passenger planes for a number of years before Freddy Laker began to acquire them for his new project. June 21st 1961 saw the first test flight of the Carvair and seven months later, with Captain Dudley Scorge at the controls, the first scheduled Carvair flight from Southend Airport to Ostend took off. Scheduled services later also ran to Calais, Le Touquet, Strasbourg, Rotterdam, Basle and Geneva and also departed from Lydd, in Kent, and Bournemouth.

The airline business was very fickle and seasonal demand fluctuated wildly. Routes and timetables were constantly changed and scheduled services eventually ended in 1979. The aircraft were then leased to different operators and their uses varied wildly including such tasks as Red Cross relief work, flying pop artists and their gear to concerts, civil engineering contracts in the Middle East and of course flying Goldfinger's props back and forth to Switzerland. With so many different operators, and liveries frequently changing there were concerns about the extra weight of too many layers of paint.

The first Carvairs had sober names such as *Zeeland* or *Golden Gate Bridge*. Later they were given names more suited to their unique characteristics like *Porky Pete, Big Louie* (later to be called *Plane Jane*), *Fat Annie, Barb and Fat Albert*. As the years passed the Carvair fleet shrank. Six were written off as the result of accidents. At the end of the Vietnam War a Carvair named *Barb* was damaged by mortar fire in Phnom Penn, Cambodia. It was abandoned on the airfield and left as a decoy target. Another Carvair, in service for the Red Cross, was impounded in Bangkok; one was retired and turned into a restaurant in the Dominican Republic. A number of the older models were withdrawn from service and cannibalised for spares.

At the time of writing only one Carvair is left, (no 21) the last one to be built, which is in storage in South Africa. In the UK there is very little in the way of memorabilia save for some old photographs and of course the film clip from Goldfinger.

Freddy Laker had an earlier dream. It was to build a dual purpose twin propeller cargo/passenger plane to compete with the World War II work horse, the Douglas DC3. This was the aircraft that carried thousands of paratroopers during the D. Day invasion and the Arnhem landings. Laker named this aircraft the Accountant. It was designed by a dedicated

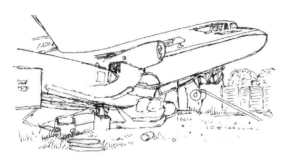

team based at ATL at Southend Airport. Unfortunately designing an aircraft from scratch is expensive and as the work progressed costs spiralled. The one and only prototype aircraft registered as G-41-1 took to the air in July 1957. Yet there were few buyers.

The price of the Accountant was considerably more than the DC3. Early in 1958, after taking advice from ATL's accountants, Freddy Laker reluctantly scrapped the Accountant. Skulduggery on the part of rival aircraft manufacturers was alleged but nothing could be substantiated.

A surviving photograph shows the aircraft re-registered G-ATEL, partially dismantled and unceremoniously dumped on the side of Southend airport in 1960. Since then the Accountant has been heard of no more.

WRITING ON THE WALL

If you ever come to Walden by the single track,
You're advised to place your luggage firmly in the rack,
And walk the two odd miles at a steady easy pace,
For it will prove the quickest way of getting to the place.

One hundred years separated the two great eras of railways. The 1860s saw railway building on an unprecedented scale and the 1960s saw a ruthless closure programme. The branch line between Audley End and Saffron Walden was involved in both.

Saffron Walden's branch line opened in 1865. The town council had recommended a link to the London to Cambridge route five years earlier. The necessary capital was raised and parliamentary approval granted. However, even before construction began, there was dissent amongst the directors about extending the line further north to Bartlow. Work on the northern extension proved more challenging due to the hilly terrain as the line approached Bartlow.

Finances were stretched, nevertheless the extension was finished 11 months later and by October 1866 the line was in operation along its full length. If nothing else the Victorian railway builders were determined to get their project completed and paid little heed to environmental or archaeological concerns. They were quite content to bulldoze anything that got in the way as was witnessed in the destruction of the Roman barrows at Bartlow. The line was beset with problems from the start. Passenger numbers were less than anticipated and within 10 years the Saffron Walden Railway Company sold out to avoid bankruptcy.

After the Second World War Britain's railways were taken into state ownership. Yet in spite of receiving large amounts from the taxpayer they continued to lose money, passengers and freight. The government's attitude was changing too and railways were no longer seen as the backbone of the economy. Trains were a burden and a financial liability. Motor transport and roads were perceived as the country's future.

In 1961, Dr Richard Beeching was appointed as chairman of British Rail with a task of stemming the losses. His solution was to close 4,000 miles of rail line and 3,000 stations. The plan was put into effect and completed over a 10 year period. The Saffron Walden Branch line was an early casualty in what was known as the Beeching Axe.

Saffron Waldon's last passenger train was the 8.09pm Sunday night service and ran on 7th September 1964. To a certain extent it is surprising the service lasted that long. The 'Writing on the Wall' had been up for sometime, as seen in the edited verse above which was sent by a disgruntled passenger known as CM to a local paper fifteen years earlier.

PIRATES
MY SHIP IS COMING IN

A vicious snow laden wind hit the ship,
The mooring stretched, strained and began to rip.

Wednesday evening, January 19th 1966, the weather on the east coast of Essex was bleak. It was cold and stormy with flurries of snow. Out at sea, four miles off Frinton and just beyond British territorial waters, lay the *Mi Amigo*, a converted cargo boat and home of the 'pirate' radio station, *Radio Caroline*.

Below decks most of the staff, engineers and disc jockeys, including Dave Lee Travis and Tony Blackburn, watched television. They were completely oblivious to the fact that the ship had broken its anchor chain and was being blown towards the shore. Only when a volunteer (Travis) was needed to adjust the television aerial, a regular occurrence that required going on deck, was something judged amiss. Hastily all the DJs, engineers and crew mustered in the lounge with their life jackets ready to hand. Almost immediately there was a great crash and everybody was thrown over as the ship hit the beach broadside on. Fortunately it came to rest between two metal breakwaters. Maybe it was prophetic but the number two on *Radio Caroline's* chart that week was 'My Ship is Coming in' by the Walker Brothers.

Radio Caroline had started broadcasting nearly two years earlier when DJ Simon Dee, aboard the Motor Vessel *Fredrica* (predecessor of the *Mi Amigo*) uttered the following words; "Hello everybody. This is *Radio*

Caroline, broadcasting on 199, your all-day music station". Today it is difficult to imagine what little choice listeners had then in the way of broadcast music. Prior to the arrival of *Radio Caroline,* what now is classed as pop music was only continuously available from foreign stations such *Radio Luxembourg,* which tended to fade out at night, or *Radio Veronica,* a Dutch 'pirate' anchored off the coast of Holland.

Radio Veronica's transmissions were aimed at a Dutch audience, consequently its language was Dutch, although most of the music played was English and American from the popular charts of the day. Even so its broadcasts could be heard over much of Eastern England, providing a stark contrast to the dull music offerings available from the BBC which had a monopoly in the UK. In the sixties the British government strongly opposed 'pirate' broadcasting; citing interference with safety of shipping and emergency wavebands as well as imagined harmful effects on the population at large among other things.

It was not on a whim that the first offshore stations were moored off the Essex coast. With their powerful transmitters they were strategically placed to reach audiences in London, East Anglia and the Midlands. In spite of government threats and efforts at discouragement, millions of people tuned in to these new broadcasters. *Radio London* quickly joined *Caroline,* and then *Radio England, Britain Radio* and even a *Radio Essex* took to the airwaves. Soon the waters off Essex were crowded with wannabee broadcasters.

The government continued with threats of action against illegal activity on the high seas but did little. It was left to the weather to do the job for them, which brings us back to the events on that stormy evening of Wednesday, January 19th, 1966. A heroic effort by local lifeboat crews ensured the survival of the illustrious DJs and all those aboard.

Radio Caroline was back on the air within two months but the days of the 'pirates' were numbered. One of the pirate stations, *Radio City,* was based on Shivering Sands, an old World War II fort in the Thames estuary. A dispute between rivals about the ownership of its assets resulted in Reg Calvert, the boss of Radio City, being shot dead at his home in Wendens Ambo near Saffron Walden.

With this killing the government now had the excuse it needed and acted swiftly on the grounds that pirate radio was being run by gangsters. In 1967 the Marine Offences Act came into effect which resulted in the closing of all the offshore stations with the notable exception of *Radio Caroline*. The broadcasts continued intermittently from the *Mi Amigo* until March 1980 when, during a storm, the 60 year old ship, which by then was barely seaworthy, sank after running aground on the Long Sand Bank. The crew were all taken off unharmed.

Six weeks after the new law was enacted the BBC introduced its own national pop music station, Radio 1, with none other than Tony Blackburn at the helm.

Radio Caroline washed ashore. All survived.

Although the *Mi Amigo* was gone *Radio Caroline* resurrected itself in 1983 and started broadcasting offshore from a new vessel, the converted trawler *Ross Revenge*. In November 1991 this too was abandoned during a gale and ran aground on the Goodwin Sands. Unlike the *Mi Amigo*, it was later salvaged and restored in Tilbury Docks. The *Ross Revenge* is now moored in the River Blackwater. *Radio Caroline*, no longer a 'pirate', broadcasts completely legally and can be heard via satellite and on online.

ESSEX BOYS

It was 2 to 1 up with seconds to go.
Then as tension built came a terrible blow.
Germany scored and snatched the match back.
The England team was now on the rack.

WEMBLEY, 30ᵀᴴ JULY 1966, WORLD CUP FINAL RESULT - ENGLAND 4, WEST GERMANY 2.

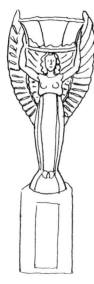

The result might have been written - Essex 4, Germany 2, since a quartet of 'Essex Boys' played a crucial role in the outcome. The team manager, Alf Ramsay, came from Dagenham and the Captain, Bobby Moore, who accepted the *Jules Rimet* trophy for England from the Queen, was a Barking lad. Martin Peters, who scored one of the goals, was from Plaistow, and Geoff Hurst, the hero of the match who scored the other three goals, was considered an honorary Essex Boy since he had spent his best playing years at West Ham.

It was a hot summer's day as the match got under way. After thirteen minutes West Germany took the lead but six minutes later Geoff Hurst, connecting with a Bobby Moore free kick, headed the ball home to level the score. England then took the lead when a deflection from Hurst (again) enabled Martin Peters to smash the ball into goal with his right foot. As the seconds ticked towards the end of normal time, disaster struck when the Germans equalised with virtually the last kick of the game.

The talk by Alf Ramsay at the break between full time and extra time was inspirational in lifting the team's spirits. He refused to let them dwell on tiredness and disappointment. Pointing to the German players he shouted "look at them, they're finished!" The manager then eyed his men and spoke calmly saying; "All right - you let it slip - now start again". The team's spirits were lifted.

Shortly after extra time started Geoff Hurst scored his second goal with a strong shot that bounced on the underside of the crossbar. The German team hotly disputed the goal, the referee was unsure, but the linesman was positive and the goal stood.

There was no doubt about the fourth goal, as in the dying seconds of the game Geoff Hurst picked up yet another pass from Bobby Moore and blasted a shot in from 25 yards. As Hurst was running down the left wing some spectators had come onto the pitch. This prompted Kenneth Wolstenholme, the BBC commentator, looking at the crowd, to excitedly shout into the microphone "Some of the crowd are on the pitch, they think it's all over," then as Hurst's shot hit the roof of the net he completed the sentence with "It is now". These words have become part of footballing legend and are almost as famous as the result itself.

Alf Ramsay, England's most successful manager, was knighted in 1970. He suffered a stroke during the 1998 world cup finals and died in 1999. Bobby Moore, manager of Southend United between 1984 and 1986, died of cancer in 1993.

Geoff Hurst was knighted in 1998; both he and Martin Peters were given the MBE for services to football.

LET IT ROCK!

1000s came on foot or by bus, car, train or ferry
And it wasn't to Woodstock, Reading or Glastonbury.
From Friday to Bank Holiday Monday it was non-stop rock
With dozens of bands playing around the clock.

The committee of the Clacton Round Table did not know what they were letting themselves in for when they settled on a proposal before them to replace the 'Annual Donkey Derby' with a different charity fund raiser. Perhaps inadvertently staging one of the biggest rock concerts ever seen in the British Isles wasn't exactly what they had in mind. However that is exactly what happened at Weeley, in Essex, over the August Bank Holiday weekend in 1971.

Advanced purchase tickets for the three-day event were offered at £1.50 and the gate entry price was £2.00. The organisers thought they would do well, with half a dozen local bands, to get an audience of maybe five, maximum ten, thousand. It was an event planned long before the days of the internet, e-mails or mobile phones. Yet, as the Bank Holiday weekend approached, hundreds of people began turning up in the Weeley area and camping out. They came from all over the country. Having seen small advertisements in the music press or heard by word of mouth, they travelled to Essex by any means possible.

Fortunately the Round Tablers realised in advance that the event was growing exponentially so allowed a professional promoter to look after the bands. No longer were only a rag tag of local musicians billed to appear but alongside them 36 acts were named on the entry ticket alone. These included a pick of the popular musical celebrities of the day such as Rod Stewart, Lindisfarne, T. Rex, Edgar Brown, Mungo Jerry, Dave Edmunds and Juicy Lucy.

By the time the first band was due to play at 10.00pm on the Friday an estimated crowd of 100,000 was packed into the site and still more were arriving all the time. At its peak upwards of 150,000 were thought to have attended. The organisers even appealed for no one else to come but the message didn't get out or, if it did, it wasn't heeded. It now became a free concert, as it was almost impossible and probably dangerous to try to collect gate money. The great majority who were there spoke of how wonderful it was. There was some trouble between caterers the 'Pie Men' and the self-appointed security guards, the 'Hells Angels', but in general Essex Police reported only a few arrests and localised parking difficulties.

Alas the Clacton Round Table collected little or no money for the good causes and in fact they were lucky not to have been landed with a huge bill for clearing up. One local farmer collected an unusual souvenir. A double decker bus, used for hospitality and as a changing room for the bands, was left behind by the promoter, who subsequently declined to collect it.

THE ENTERPRISE HAS LANDED

It was Stansted's biggest crowd puller to date
And perhaps 250,000 visitors passed through the gate?
'The Enterprise' was what they'd all come to see,
On the fifth of June nineteen-eighty-three.

The first 'reusable' manned space vehicle to orbit the earth was the space shuttle *Colombia*. Its maiden flight took place in April 1981. However, before the space shuttle could go into space, it was necessary to prove that it could land back on earth. A specially commissioned prototype space shuttle orbiter was used to test free flight landing procedures. This was called OV101, or more commonly, the *Enterprise*.

Two years later, following the first successful space shuttle flights, the American National Aeronautics and Space Administration (NASA) decided to send the Enterprise on a world-wide promotional tour. Stansted was its first port of call in Europe. Originally the proposed name of the 'shuttle' was the *Constitution*. However a massive letter writing campaign by space enthusiasts persuaded the powers that be to change it to that of the craft in the popular science fiction show *Star Trek*.

The space shuttle Enterprise landed in Essex, on 5th June 1983, at Stansted Airport. It arrived in style at 15.45, mounted piggyback on top of a modified Boeing 747 but arrived an hour late. It was a glorious sunny day, the VIPs were all seated and the spectators waited expectantly. It was to be a great photographic occasion to remember and the *Sally B*, the historic B17 World War II bomber, made a fly past before returning to nearby Duxford. Unfortunately two busloads of press photographers were unable to disembark at the right time to capture the landing moment as they were held back by over enthusiastic security personnel.

The 747 pilot, Fitzhugh Fulton of the United States Airforce, brought his plane to a stop on the concourse to tumultuous applause. The Enterprise stayed for two days. Whilst security may have spoilt the press photographer's day they seemed unable to control the numbers of spectators who turned up. Some estimates put the number of visitors at 250,000 but nobody knows for sure. Whatever the figure, the narrow country lanes around the airport became completely blocked and there was traffic chaos. Stansted airport was in its infancy and parking and the road infrastructure was not what it is today.

One of the best views of the *Enterprise* was from the air and a shrewd operator, based at Southend Airport, offered sightseeing flights using vintage Douglas DC-3 Dakotas.

Although the *Enterprise* only stayed in Essex for two days the visit was a hugely popular success. It is remembered in the corporate address of Stansted Airport, Enterprise House, named in honour of the shuttle's visit. On site there is also a meeting room called the Fulton, named after the chief pilot Fitzhugh Fulton.

The Enterprise was built as a test vehicle and was not equipped for, and therefore never experienced, space flight. It is now housed in a museum just outside Washington DC in the 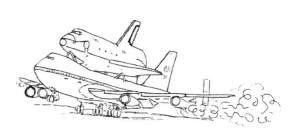 USA. The original fully fledged space shuttle *Colombia*, the first shuttle to fly in space, disintegrated during re-entry on its 28th mission, on 1 February 2003. All seven crew members aboard perished. The 5th June 2008 marked the 25th Anniversary of the shuttle's visit to Essex. To mark the occasion Derek Winter of BBA Stansted organised a special reunion celebration in Enterprise House including the making of an 'Enterprise' cake. 2008 also marked the 50th anniversary of NASA.

LAMBS TO THE SLAUGHTER

1,000 people faced the driver on that first night
Having been out since dawn to exert their right.

It all began on 16th January 1995. It 'ended' on Monday 30th October. For nine months the small Essex town of Brightlingsea had been traumatised by the events that took place. One man had died, 598 people had been arrested and 1,200 complaints had been made against the police. Thousands of pounds worth of damage had been inflicted on the port area and the cost of policing during all this was estimated at five million pounds. Many protesters had lost their jobs and businesses had been ruined. It would take a long time for all the wrongs to be put right and longer for the psychological scars to be healed.

At the centre of the conflict that produced all this fury was the export of live animals to the continent, especially lambs and veal calves. The trade had been going on for years but with increasing difficulty for exporters. A growing, and increasingly militant, animal rights movement was completely opposed to it and the harsh conditions in which the animals were transported. It was the latter, the unacceptable and inhumane way the animals were transported, that drew an even wider public support to the protest.

Many ports such as Shoreham, Plymouth, Dover and Kings Lynn had already faced the fury of demonstrators and ceased shipments. As a result Brightlingsea, almost by default, became the chosen place for a showdown. A determined exporter and a cooperative port owner had joined forces. After all the Government, in the shape of DEFRA* had ruled that, notwithstanding that the welfare of animals was paramount, this was a lawful trade. During the course of ten months 174 convoys carrying 150,000 sheep and 60,000 veal calves passed through Brightlingsea. The animals were then shipped to Belgium on the *MV Caroline*. (There was no connection with the pirate radio station of the same name.)

Protesters, often numbered in their thousands, made determined

Lucky the Lamb,
The One That Got Away

efforts to halt the shipments. At times the police invoked the public order act and several injunctions were taken out against leading protesters. On occasions the demonstration turned violent when tempers were lost. The ranks of the protesters, largely peaceful but vociferous, were swollen at times by agitators whose sole purpose was to cause trouble and violence. In their turn the police were frequently accused of heavy handedness.

There appeared to be no winners except perhaps one. A sheep was 'kidnapped' from the port by protesters and christened 'Lucky the Lamb'. Lucky never went to Belgium and presumably survived to a ripe old age.

WINDMILLS ON MY MIND

From Dagenham's industrial heartland they creep,
Across Essex, to the sea. They never sleep.

Windmills have been in Essex for more than 600 years, primarily used for pumping water or grinding flour, they were once very much part of the landscape. Traditional windmills were basically of three types. First were the post mills, so named because of the large upright post on which the mill's main structure balanced. This allowed the whole mill to rotate according to the wind direction. Bocking Mill near Braintree, built in 1721, is a good example.

The next development was the smock mill. The smock mill that remains in Upminster was built in 1803 by local farmer, James Noake. The name is attributed to their resemblance to the smocks worn by most farm labourers of the day. The wooden body of this type of mill no longer rotated, only the cap holding the sails turned to follow the wind.

Lastly came, tower mills. They were a refinement of the smock mill. The wooden body was replaced with a fixed brick or stone built tower. A lovingly restored tower mill, originally put up in 1816, may be seen standing in the village of Stock.

Working windmills reached their greatest numbers in the 1830s. Thirty years later many were struggling to survive. They progressively had to compete with more reliable power sources, coal-fired steam engines then oil-burning engines, followed by electricity from the national grid. The agricultural depressions of the late nineteenth century added to the windmills' hardships and hundreds were forced to close. Many were demolished or just abandoned. By 1950 most had ceased to be used commercially, unable to compete with factory production methods. Many of the windmills we see today owe their existence to their status as heritage attractions maintained by bands of volunteers.

In the 1970s however the manufacturing technology that led to the demise of the windmill was itself subject to threat. Its power source had become totally reliant upon OIL! The 1973 Arab oil embargo, as a result of the Arab-Israeli war, sent shock waves across the west. The price of oil rocketed and there were fears for future supplies. Together with growing concerns over the effect of burning fossil fuels on the planet's environment alternative energy sources were needed.

In 1957 construction commenced in Essex on what was to become Britain's first fully commercial nuclear plant power. The station at Bradwell was built on the wartime 'Bradwell Bay' airfield on the coast of the Dengie peninsula on the Blackwater estuary. Electricity generation started in 1962. In the late 1950s and early 60s nuclear power was considered to be clean, reliable, enduring and above all cheap. Bradwell was a Magnox station. Magnox is short for magnesium non-oxidising but the system soon became obsolete and Bradwell seldom achieved its planned output. Soon concerns soon grew about safety and the problems of dealing satisfactorily with nuclear waste. Fears became acute after the 1979 accident at Three Mile Island in the USA and the 1986 Chernobyl disaster in the former Soviet Union.

In 1999, British Nuclear Fuels announced that Bradwell was no longer economic to operate and would cease operation in 2002. The controversy that has surrounded nuclear power was maybe visible in microcosm when the gates finally closed at Easter 2002. Assembled on one side was a small group of people, looking close to tears, whilst on the other side was another group applauding and clapping.

The wheel seemed to have turned full circle and windmills in the form of wind turbines were looked to as a possible solution. In 2004 the Ford Motor Company erected two wind turbines at Dagenham which they say generate enough power to meet the needs of their state of the art Diesel Assembly Hall. Each turbine is nearly the same height as the London Eye, 120 metres tall. The design principle used is the same as the old smock mill where the metal tower is fixed. The cap that houses the generator and carries the turbine blades rotates according to wind direction. A third turbine has since been added at Dagenham.

Whilst wind turbines are a familiar site across much of Essex they have proved controversial and attract almost as much opposition as nuclear power. On the Dengie peninsula several wind farm schemes have been abandoned or curtailed due to determined local protest.

Wind farms at sea off of the Essex coast have proved less contentious although they are more costly to construct and operate but do have great potential.

If the wheel really has turned full circle for wind power then windmills may well be here for another 600 years or so. Whether they will be commercially viable then or just heritage landmarks is another matter.

THE ESSEX COAT OF ARMS

The Seaxes

Throughout Essex the county coat of arms appears on village and town signs, school name boards, fire engines, police helmets and county council vehicles.

The coat of arms consists of three seaxes placed one above the other. The seax is a curved sword or knife with a hilt, its handle terminating in a pommel or knob. There is a semi-circular notch on the back of each blade and they are believed to have evolved from Saxon short swords which were originally 21 – 46 cms long and about 5 cms deep. The official coat of arms description is:- Gules, three Seaxes fessewise in pale Argen, pommels (knobs) and hilts (handles) pointed to the sinister and cutting edges upwards. In plain English this is; silver seaxes shown horizontally with the cutting edge upwards and the pommel pointing to the left, shown on a red shield.

There is an element of mystery as to why Essex adopted the seax. In *the Anglo Saxon Chronicles* Essex is called Eastseaxe. Studies by historians and heraldic experts suggest something similar to the Essex coat of arms was used in the East Saxon kingdom over 1,000 years ago. The Saxons were decisively defeated by King Knut's (Canute) Danish Vikings at the Battle of Ashingdon in 1016. King Canute became the undisputed King of England and the Saxon rulers fled west or went into exile. Although the Saxons returned following the death of King Canute they were again crushed by the Normans in the Battle of Hastings in 1066.

The Essex coat of arms appeared in print more or less as it is today, but with a Saxon crown above it, in John Speed's 1623 book *Historie of Great Britaine*. It would seem safe to assume that it was in use long before that. With the growth of printing more and more Essex towns, villages and organisations adopted the emblem. Surprisingly it was not until 1932 that the College of Arms officially granted Essex its current coat of arms.

THE ESSEX WAY

From Epping through Ongar and Fyfield go
Past Willingale's two churches - Spain and Doe.
Through Good Easter, past Pleshey's old Motte and Bailey
To Great Waltham, Terling and up to White Notley.
Now Cressing's Barns where Knights Templar once stayed,
A short walk to Coggeshall and the journey's half made.
By way of Great Tey, West Bergholt and Boxted
Arrive at Dedham where Constable once painted.
After Mistley, Manningtree, Ramsey and Little Oakley
Reach Harwich the end of this eighty-one mile journey.

The Essex Way is a long distance footpath that meanders north west across the county starting at London's Central Line tube station at Epping and continuing to the port of Harwich.

At Epping the outlaw Dick Turpin laid low in the forest. A few miles further along Willingale's two churches stand side by side on the same plot of land, but no squabbling sisters are to be seen. The footpath passes through Pleshey, mentioned in William Shakespeare's Richard II. Leaving Pleshey, the route traverses lands and manors formerly owned by the dynastic de Vere family and then by Essex bad boy Richard Riche. At Cressing the original Knights Templars' granary barns still stand. Following the River Blackwater is the halfway point of the journey, Coggeshall.

Fortunately the gang that once terrorised the area has long gone. Continuing, the Essex Way runs close to Boxted Hall where Edward III once spent the night on a secret assignation much to the chagrin of the citizens of Colchester. From Boxted the way enters Constable Country passing right by John Constable's old school in Dedham. A few miles further on, nestling the banks of the River Stour, the old Manningtree haunts of the Witch-Finder General, Matthew Hopkins reveal themselves. Just outside the town, legions of swans boldly strut up and down. Their ancestors would have much to tell if questioned. Richard Rigby's great folly, the twin towers at Mistley, loom into view. Following the banks of the Stour to Harwich, on the North Sea coast, the 81 miles of the Essex Way end at the high lighthouse. The port was once the Parliamentary seat of Samuel Pepys and the birthplace of exploring sea captains. Stunning scenery, mystery, intrigue, adventure and years of history - the Essex Way has them all.

LOCATIONS AND CONTACT ADDRESSES
(By subject)

Armageddon
Kelvedon Hatch Secret Nuclear Bunker
Kelvedon Hall Lane
Great Myles Ongar Road
Kelvedon Hatch CM14 5TZ www.secretnuclearbunker.com

Billericay Pioneers
Cater Museum
74 High Street
Billericay Essex
CM12 9BS www.catermuseum.co.uk

Boudica and Under Seige
Colchester Castle Museum, Castle Park
Colchester CO1 1YG
www.cimuseums.org.uk

It's Not Cricket / I Have a Body of a Weak and Feeble Woman
Tilbury Fort
No 2 Office Block,
The Fort, Tilbury, Essex, RM18 7NR Tel: 01375 858489

Dunmow Flitch and Doctor's Pond
Great Dunmow Museum, Mill Lane
Dunmow, Essex, CM6 1BG
www.greatdunmowmuseum.org.uk www.dunmowflitchtrials.co.uk

The Duke of Boulogne
Mountfitchet Castle
Stansted Mountfitchet
Essex CM24 8SP www.mountfitchetcastle.com

Dutch Cottage Museum
Canvey Road, Canvey Island
SS8 0QD

Essex Farm/The Essex Regiment
Chelmsford Museum and the Essex Regiment Museum
Oaklands Park, Moulsham Street, Chelmsford, CM2 9AQ
Tel: 01245 605700 www.chelmsford.gov.uk/museums

Family Courtauld
Braintree District Museum
Manor St, Braintree, CM7 3HT
www.braintreemuseum.co.uk

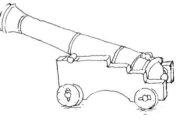

Gunpowder Mills
Waltham Abbey
Beaulieu Dr, Waltham Abbey EN9 1JX
Tel: 01992 707370
www.royalgunpowdermills.com

John Constable's School Days
Bridge Cottage, Flatford Mill
Flatford Rd, East Bergholt, Suffolk CO7 6UL
01206 298260

Just Mad about Saffron
Uttlesford Tourist and Community Information Centre
1 Market Place, Saffron Walden, Essex CB10 1HR
Tel: 01799 524002

Layer Marney Tower /Loyal Subject
Maldon Road, (Signposted from B1022)
Layer Marney, Colchester CO5 9US, www.layermarneytower.co.uk

Longer than a Mile
Southend Visitor Information Centre
Southend Pier, Western Esplanade,
Southend-on-Sea Essex SS1 1EE Tel. 01702 618747

Magna Carta (de Vere)/ Shakespeare
Hedingham Castle
Bayley St, Castle Hedingham, Essex. CO9 3DJ
Tel: 01787 460261 www.hedinghamcastle.co.uk

Not a lot of people know that.
Waltham Abbey Tourist Information Centre
6 Highbridge Street
Waltham Abbey, Essex, EN9 1DG Tel 01992 660336

Plotlanders
Essex Wildlife Trust Ltd
Langdon Nature Reserve, Third Av,
Basildon SS16 6EB
Tel: 01268 419103

Salvation Army Colony
Salvation Army, Hadleigh Farm
Castle Lane, Benfleet SS7 2AP
www.hadleighfarm.co.uk

Sea Witch, Leigh Fishy Tales, Little Ships of Leigh
Leigh Heritage Centre
13a High Street
Leigh-On-Sea SS9 2EN

Stow Maries Great War Aerodrome
Flambards Chase
Hackman's Lane
Purleigh, Nr Maldon,
Essex CM3 6RJ   www.stowmaries.org.uk

Thames Barge
Maldon District Tourist Information Centre
High St, Maldon, Essex CM9 5AD
01621 856503 www.visitmaldondistrict.co.uk

Thaxted
Thaxted Community Information
7 Town Street, Thaxted, Essex, CM6 2LD
Tel: 01371 831641

Three Days that shook the Kingdom
Brentwood Tourist Information Centre
44 High Street, Brentwood CM14 4AJ Phone: 01277 312500

Tiptree Jam
Wilkin & Sons Limited
Church Road, Tiptree CO5 0RF
Tel: 01621 814524 www.trooms.com

Walton Tower/ Rigby's Follies

Naze Tower, The Naze,
Old Hall Lane, Walton-on-the-Naze,
Essex CO14 8LE Tel: 01255 852519
www.nazetower.co.uk

Waterway to Chelmsford

Paper Mill Lock, North Hill, Little Baddow,
Chelmsford, Essex, CM3 4BS Tel: 01245 225520
www.papermilllock.co.uk

William Byrd

Ingatestone Hall
Hall Lane, Hall Lane, Ingatestone Hall
Essex, CM4 9NR Tel 01277 353010 www.ingatestonehall.com

William Morris

William Morris Gallery
Lloyd Park, Forest Road
Walthamstow, London, E17 4PP
Tel: 020 8496 4390 www.wmgallery.org.uk

Whilst every care has been taken to ensure the accuracy of the above information the editors are unable to accept responsibility for its content which has been supplied in good faith.

ABOUT THE AUTHORS

ANDREW SUMMERS

Born within the sound of Bow Bells on a quiet day, Andrew has lived for the last 25 years in Hadleigh and been married to Glenis for 48 years. Andrew has bought books, sold books, printed books and now decided to write and publish books too! Separately Andrew has edited *The Number Had to Tally* a Second World War survival story and written *They Did Their Duty, Essex Farm* which tells the story of Essex Farm in Belgium and its connections with the Essex Regiment.

JOHN DEBENHAM

Born in Romford John has always lived in Essex. On retirement from engineering he took a BA History degree followed by an MA in Intellectual History, studying 'Civilisation and Barbarism' and continues to enjoy historical research. A member of Southend Poetry Society he writes poetry and short stories with longer works in 'perpetual progress'.

AND THE ARTIST: ELIZABETH SUMMERS

Elizabeth lives in Suffolk. She has illustrated several books apart from those in the Essex Hundred series. Elizabeth's latest work include illustrations for books written by children's author and former French tennis Grand Slam champion and Wimbledon finalist Christine Truman.

AND THE CONTRIBUTING POETS

SHIRLEY BAKER - (Dunmow Flitch, Tiptree Jam, Harbingers at Harlow, Dutch Cottage, Walton Tower, Missing Person from Harlow and The Little Ships of Leigh) Shirley lives in Leigh-on-Sea, Essex and has been writing for many years. She is a member of the Southend Poetry Group and has published poems on a wide variety of subjects. Shirley had also written *Aeolus Ruler of the Winds* a delightful east coast sailing book.

JOHN F BARR - (Happy Harry) Born in Essex John worked as a Chartered Surveyor until retiring in 2005. He has had several poems published in the Southend Poetry Group's anthologies.

CHRISTINE BILLINGTON - (William Morris) Writing since a teenager Christine has had several collections of poetry published by K.T. Publications and many pieces taken by small press publishers.

CLARE HARVEY - (Joscelyne's Beach Chalkwell) Born in Wiltshire, but of an old Leigh bloodline, since retirement, in 2001, Clare concentrates on 5 grandchildren, poetry, photography, painting, gardening, swimming and long term partner - Mervyn!

MERVYN LINFORD - (Three Mills at Battlesbridge and Mulberry) Mervyn has been writing for over thirty years. He has had work published in many magazines, periodicals and anthologies and has been broadcast on both local and national radio. He has had seven collections of poetry published and four works of prose. He runs the 'Littoral Press' and is Poetry Editor for 'Pentangle' magazine.

KATIE MALLETT - (Coalhouse Fort) Katie has written poems and articles since the 1980s. Her work has appeared in Essex magazines and newspapers, and various anthologies, including a series of books edited by E.O. Parrott published by Penguin/Viking. She was BBC Essex resident Poet for 5 years before moving to North Devon in 2005.

ADRIAN GREEN - (Sweyn's Castle) Adrian Green lives overlooking the sea at Southend. He holds degrees in psychology and general arts as well as a Post Graduate Diploma in Humanities. He is a former editor of SOL magazine, and reviews editor of Littoral Press. He has published 2 pamphlet collections – 'Beachgame' and 'The Watchers'. His most recent book 'Chorus and Coda' was published in 2007.

MARGARET RICE - (Witch-Finder General) Margaret, who died in 2006, had a love of language and literature throughout her life. A move to Essex in 2003 focused her writing and particularly poetry allowing her to produce some of her most observant and poignant work.

ESSEX HUNDRED PUBLICATIONS

Essex Hundred Publications publishes, in the main, a range of Essex centred local history books. A selection can be seen on pages 212 and 213. By Essex we mean not just the county of Essex as it is today but also the areas of Essex that have been absorbed into London since 1965. The company also distributes a range of local history books from other publishers and has a large portfolio of Essex images. Essex Hundred authors are also happy to give talks on the subjects published. For further details consult www.essex100.com or e-mail ask@essex100.com

SELECTED BIBLIOGRAPHY

Addison, William, *Essex Worthies : a biographical companion to the County*, Phillimore, 1973.

Adkin, Mark, *The Trafalgar Companion*, Aurum Press Ltd, 2005.

Anderson, Mark, *Shakespeare by Another Name*, Gotham Books, 2006.

Anderson, Verily, *The de Veres of Castle Hedingham*, Terence Dalton, 1993.

Backscheider, Paula, R., *Daniel Defoe*, John Hopkins University, 1989.

Basildon Branch Libraries, *Billericay and the New World: a summary*, Essex County Library, 1970.

Bailey, Anthony, *John Constable, a Kingdom of His Own*, Chatto & Windus, 2006.

Baron, Dennis, *De Vere is Shakespeare*, The Oleander Press, 1997.

Benham, Hervey, *Some Essex Water Mills*, Essex County Newspapers Ltd, 1976.

Benham, Hervey, *The Smuggler's Century: The Story of Smuggling on the Essex Coast 1750 – 1830*, Essex Record Office Publications, 1986.

Bingley, Randal, *Fobbing, Life and Landscape,* Thurrock Museum, 1997.

Bingley, Randal, *Panorama* Thurrock Local History Society, various 1985 - 2007.

Booth William General, *In Darkest England,* Charles Knight and Co. Ltd., 1970.

Brewer, John, *Sentimental Murder,* Harper Perennial, 2005.

Bush, Reg, *Sandon A Village History,* Reg Bush, 1999.

Caffrey, Kate, *The Mayflower,* Andre Deutsch, 1975.

Carney, Terry, *Thurrock in the Thirties,* Thurrock Museum Publications, 2005.

Carpenter R.J., *Christopher Martin Great Burstead and The Mayflower,* Barnstable Books, 1982.

Carter, Douglas, *Short History of Boxted,* 1996.

Carter, M.H., *The Fort of Othona and the Chapel of St Peter-on-the-Wal,.* Provost and Chapter of Chelmsford, 1966.

Chelmsford Museum Service, *Guglielmo Marconi, 1874-1937 : The Father of Wireless.* Chelmsford Museum Service, 1987.

Chisenhale-Marsh, T.C.(Trans.), *Domesday Book relating to Essex.* W.D. Burrell, 1864.

Clark, Dr. Michael, *Rochford Hall : the history of a Tudor house and biographies of its owners,* Alan Sutton, 1990.

Colthorpe, M and Bateman, *L.H. Queen Elizabeth I and Harlow.* Harlow Development Corporation, 1997.

Coote, Stephen, *Samuel Pepys a Life,* Sceptre Hodder & Stoughton, 2001.

Currie, I. Davidson, M. Ogley, R. *The Essex Weather Book,* Froglets, 1992.

Davis, G. R. C., *Magna Carta,* British Museum, 1965.

Dean, William, P., *The ATL-98 Carvair,* McFarland & Co Inc, 2008.

Dudley, Donald.R, *The Rebellion of Boudicca,* Routledge and Kegan Paul, 1962.

Dury, John, *A History of Felsted*, John Dury, 1999.

Egerton, Judy, *Turner The Fighting Temeraire,* National Gallery Publications, 1995.

Embleton, Paul, *Around Stansted Mountfitchet,* Tempus Publishing, 1999.

Federation of Essex Womens Institutes (Compiled by), *Essex Village Book,* Countryside, 2001.

Garwood, Ivan, *Mistley in the days of the Rigbys,* Lucas Books, 2003.

Gould, Rev. Sabine Baring-Gould, *Mehalah,* Boydell, 1983.

Green, Georgina, *The Story of Hainault Forest,* London Borough of Redbridge Library Services, 2001.

Grieve, Hilda, *The Sleepers and the Shadows, Volumes I and II,* Essex Records Office, 1988 and 1994.

Grun, Bernard, *The Timetables of History,* Simon and Schuster, 1982.

Hallman, Robert, *South Benfleet a History,* Phillimore, 2005.

Hartcup, Guy, *Code Name Mulberry,* David and Charles, 1977.

Humphries, Ralph, C. *Radio Caroline: the pirate years.* Oakwood, 2003.

Jacobs, Norman, *Clacton on Sea: a Pictorial History,* Phillimore, 1993.

Jarvis, Stan, *Smuggling in East Anglia 1700 – 1840,* Countryside Books, 1987.

Johns, Adrian, *Death of a Pirate,* W. W. Norton & Company, 2011.

Jones, Phil, *The Siege of Colchester 1648,* Tempus Publishing Ltd, 2003.

Joscelyne, Arthur, *Joscelyne's beach : a memoir of Leigh-on-Sea,* Desert Island Books, 2004.

Joscelyne, Arthur, *Joscelyne's Tales of Old Leigh and Chalkwell,* Desert Island Books, 2005.

Killick, Jennifer, *Sea Fencibles 1805,* Jennifer Killick, 2001.

Knights, E. Spurgeon, *William Byrd and Stondon Massey : a great musician and his life in Essex,* Essex Review, 1934.

Lake, Hazel, *The Arkwrights and Harlow,* (the author)1996.

Latham, R. and Matthews,W, Eds. *The Diary of Samuel Pepys,* Bell & Hyman, 1983.

Lemmon, David & Marshall, Mike, *Essex County Cricket Club,* Kingswood Press, 1987.

Lewis, Jim, *London's Lea Valley : Britain's best kept secret,* Phillimore, 1999.

Lister, Keith, *Half My Life, The Story of Sabine Baring-Gould and Grace,* Charnwood Publications, 2002.

Lockwood, Martin, *The Coggeshall Gang,* Essex Police Museum, 1995.

MacCamley, N. J, *Cold War Secret Nuclear Bunkers,* Leo Cooper, 2002.

Male, Dr D A. and Kemp-Luck, Mrs A. (Compiled by), *From Serf to Citizen,* Harwich Town Council, 2004.

Martin, Frank, *Rogues River,* Ian Hendry, 1983.

Martin, John, *Beyond Belief. The Real Life of Daniel Defoe,* Accent Press Ltd, 2006.

Marriage, John, *Barging into Chelmsford : the story of the Chelmer and Blackwater navigation,* Ian Hendry, 1997.

Marsden, Barry M, *The Early Barrow Diggers,* Tempus, 1999.

Morgan, Glyn, *Essex Witches : the witches, enchantments, charms and sorcerers of Essex.* Spurbooks, 1973.

Morgan, Glyn, *Secret Essex,* Ian Hendry, 1994.

Morris, Richard, *The Harveys of Rolls Park Chigwell Essex,* Loughton and District Historical Society, 2005.

National Trust Local Committee, *Rayleigh Mount,* 1965.

Neale, Kenneth, *Essex 'full of profitable thinges',* Leopard's Head Press, 1996.

O'Leary, J.G, *The Book of Dagenham,* Borough of Dagenham, 1964.

Parkhill, Gordon and Cook, Graham, *Hadleigh Salvation Army Farm, A Vision Reborn,* Salvation Army Shield Books, 2008.

Pitt-Stanley, Sheila, *Legends of Leigh,* Pitt-Stanley, 1989.

Pluck, A,R, *Stow Maries, Great War Aerodrome,* Friends of Stow Maries Aerodrome, 2014.

Powles, John, *Iron in the Blood,* Tony Brown, 2005.

Pratt, Barbara, *The Loppers of Loughton,* Barbara Pratt Publications, 1981.

Price, Harry, *The Most Haunted House in England : ten years' investigation of Borley Rectory,* Chivers Press, 1975.

Rumble, Alexander, Editor, *Doomsday Book Essex,* Phillimore, 1983.

Scott, E.V, *The Best of Essex Countryside* County Guide Publications, 1976.

Scott, Winifred N, *Coryton. History of a Village,* Mobil, 1981.

Sharpe, James, *Dick Turpin - The Myth of the English Highwayman,* Profile Books, 2005.

Shepherd, E.W, *The Story of Southend Pier - and its associations,* Egon, 1979.

Sipple, Mavis, *Rochford A History,* Phillimore, 2004.

Smith, Graham, *Smuggling in Essex,* Countryside Books, 2005.

Smith, Michael. *I am just going outside: Captain Oates - Antarctic tragedy,* Spellmount, 2002.

Smith, Victor T.C, *Coalhouse Fort,* Essex County Council, 1985.

Tomalin, Claire, *Samuel Pepys The Unequalled Self,* Viking Penguin, 2002.

Vingoe, Lesley, *Hockley, Hullbridge and Hawkwell Past,* Phillimore, 1999.

Wander, Tim, *Marconi's New Street Works, 1912 – 2012,* Authors online, 2012.

Webber, Ronald, *Peasants Revolt,* Terrance Dalton,1980.

Williams, Judith, *Leigh-on-Sea: A History,* Phillimore, 2002.

Wood, Robert, *The Widow of Borley,* Duckworth, 1992.

Yearsley, Ian, *Essex Events : death, disaster, war and weather,* Phillimore, 1999.

Yearsley, Ian, *Hadleigh Past.* Phillimore, 1998.

Yearsley, Ian, *Rayleigh a History,* Phillimore, 2005.

Yearsley Ian, *History of Southend,* Phillimore, 2001.

Essex Hundred Publications
Further bibliographic details are listed in our other books particularly, *London's Metropolitan Essex, They Did Their Duty, Essex Farm* and *Magna Carta in Essex.*

Pamphlets
Steer, F.W., *The Coat of Arms of the County of Essex,* ERO Pamphlet No 2 Essex Records Office, 1949

Magazines & Newspapers.
"The Public Hell of Happy Harry" by Leslie Salisbury in *Evening Echo, November 30th, 1972.*

Full account of the calamitous earthquake in East Essex on Tuesday morning, April 22nd 1884: reprinted from *The Essex Telegraph.* Frederic Wright, 1884.

Happy Harry drawing in the crowds in Southend

Essex Hundred Publications

The Essex Hundred
The history of the county of Essex described in 100 poems
and supported with historical notes and illustrations.
A unique book written by Essex poets covering 2000 years of
county history.
ISBN: 9780955229503 £7.99

Magna Carta in Essex
Essex barons were at the forefront of those who pushed hard
for the Magna Carta, with Robert Fitzwalter, Lord of Dunmow
appointed their leader. Yet within three months of the charter
being sealed England was at war and Essex racked by conflict.
ISBN 9780993108303 £7.99

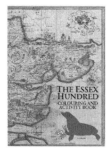

The Essex Hundred Children's Colouring and Activity Book
The Colouring and Activity Book is another title from the
Essex Hundred family aimed at children and part written by
children. The book includes not only Essex information but
pictures to colour in, word searches, puzzles and questions.
ISBN: 9780955229534 £4.99

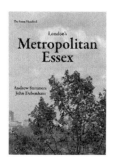

London's Metropolitan Essex
Events and Personalities, from Essex in London, which shaped
the nation's history.
ISBN 9780955229558 £12.99

Essex Hundred Publications

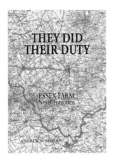

They Did Their Duty, Essex Farm, Never Forgotten by Andrew Summers
A book that tells the story of Essex Farm a First World War cemetery in Belgium that will forever bear the county name and its connections to the Essex Regiment.
ISBN 9780955229596 RRP £9.99

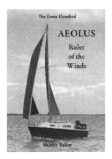

AEOLUS, Ruler of the Winds by Shirley Baker
A whimsical story of sailing adventures around the Essex and Suffolk coast.
ISBN: 9780955229589 £7.99

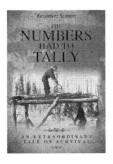

The Numbers Had to Tally by Kazimierz Szmauz
A World War II Extraordinary Tale of Survival
ISBN: 9780955229572 RRP £8.99
(digital edition available)

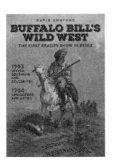

Buffalo Bill's Wild West by David Dunford
The First Reality Show in Essex
The extraordinary story of Buffalo Bill, his Wild West show and what happened when they came to Essex in the early 1900s.
ISBN 9780993108389 £7.99

FULL CIRCLE by David Dunford
The Rise, Fall and Rise of Horse Racing
in Chelmsford
ISBN 9780993108358 RRP £12.99

BATTLEFIELD ESSEX
2000 years of 'Battles' and conflicts on Essex soil
ISBN 9780993108341 RRP £8.99

Essex Hundred Publications. Books written, designed and printed in Essex.
Available from bookshops, book wholesalers, direct from the publisher
or online. **www.essex100.com**